On Regular Life, Freedom, Modernity, and Augustinian Communitarianism

READING AUGUSTINE

Series Editor:

Miles Hollingworth

In collaboration with the Wessel-Hollingworth Foundation

Reading Augustine presents books that offer personal, nuanced and oftentimes literary readings of Saint Augustine of Hippo. Each time, the idea is to treat Augustine as a spiritual and intellectual icon of the Western tradition, and to read through him to some or other pressing concern of our current day, or to some enduring issue or theme. In this way, the writers follow the model of Augustine himself, who produced his famous output of words and ideas in active tussle with the world in which he lived. When the series launched, this approach could raise eyebrows, but now that technology and pandemics have brought us into the world and society like never before, and when scholarship is expected to live the same way and responsibly, the series is well-set and thriving.

Volumes in the series:

On Music, Sense, Affect, and Voice, Carol Harrison

On Solitude, Conscience, Love and Our Inner, and Outer Lives, Ron Haflidson

On Creation, Science, Disenchantment, and the Contours of Being and Knowing,
Matthew W. Knotts

On Agamben, Arendt, Christianity, and the Dark Arts of Civilization,
Peter Iver Kaufman

On Self-Harm, Narcissism, Atonement, and the Vulnerable Christ,
David Vincent Meconi

On Faith, Works, Eternity, and the Creatures We Are, André Barbera

On Time, Change, History, and Conversion, Sean Hannan

On Compassion, Healing, Suffering, and the Purpose of the Emotional Life,
Susan Wessel

On Consumer Culture, Identity, the Church and the Rhetorics of Delight, Mark Clavier

On Creativity, Liberty, Love and the Beauty of the Law, Todd Breyfogle

On Education, Formation, Citizenship and the Lost Purpose of Learning, Joseph Clair

On Ethics, Politics and Psychology in the Twenty-First Century, John Rist

On God, The Soul, Evil and the Rise of Christianity, John Peter Kenney

On Love, Confession, Surrender and the Moral Self, Ian Clausen

On Memory, Marriage, Tears, and Meditation, Margaret R. Miles

On Mystery, Ineffability, Silence, and Musical Symbolism, Laurence Wuidar

On Regular Life, Freedom, Modernity, and Augustinian Communitarianism

Guillermo M. Jodra

BLOOMSBURY ACADEMIC
LONDON • NEW YORK • OXFORD • NEW DELHI • SYDNEY

BLOOMSBURY ACADEMIC
Bloomsbury Publishing Plc
50 Bedford Square, London, WC1B 3DP, UK
1385 Broadway, New York, NY 10018, USA
29 Earlsfort Terrace, Dublin 2, Ireland

BLOOMSBURY, BLOOMSBURY ACADEMIC and the Diana logo are trademarks
of Bloomsbury Publishing Plc

First published in Great Britain 2023

A catalogue record for this book is available from the British Library.

A catalog record for this book is available from the Library of Congress.

ISBN: HB: 978-1-3503-0353-9
PB: 978-1-3503-0352-2
ePDF: 978-1-3503-0354-6
ePUB: 978-1-3503-0355-3

Series: Reading Augustine

Typeset by Deanta Global Publishing Services, Chennai, India
Printed and bound in Great Britain

To find out more about our authors and books visit www.bloomsbury.com
and sign up for our newsletters.

CONTENTS

1

Book of Life

Book of Life

A book is what separates salvation from eternal fire. To judge our deeds, an onomasticon whose pages contain the names of those that will outlive the second and definitive death. A Book of Life enclosed in the larger Book of Creation treasuring the code of all that is and can be. Assuming that most of us would rather not be thrown into the lake of perennial fire, what do we need to do in order for our names to be found in the book that saves us from the flames? The names are written—*gegrammenon*. Will yours be found in the book when it matters most?

> Then I saw a great white throne and him who sat upon it; from his presence earth and sky fled away, and no place was found for them. And I saw the dead, great and small, standing before the throne, and books were opened. Also another book was opened, which is the book of life. And the dead were judged by what was written in the books, by what they had done. And the sea gave up the dead in it, Death and Hades gave up the dead in them, and all were judged by what they had done. Then Death and Hades were thrown into the lake of fire. This is the second death, the lake of fire; and if any one's name was not found written in the book of life, he was thrown into the lake of fire. (Revelation 20:11–15)

Who writes names in the ultimate onomasticon? Is it a feat we ought to accomplish ourselves, or is it the advent of what is to befall us? Regardless of whether we may or may not be predestined to appear in the book, there is one certainty. To avoid sharing fates with Death and Hades, our names need to be written in the Book of Life, which raises the question: If those of us still inhabiting chronology—all mortals, all humans—cannot yet contemplate the Book of Life due to the limitations of our human finitude, what does it really mean to write a life?

Writing life, writing a life, and writing about life are some of the elemental operations available to us. More often than not, when we are asked about the meaning of writing and reading lives, we reach for our predilect biography; an autobiography, perhaps. Pioneered by works such as Jean-Jacques Rousseau's 1760's *Les confessions*, the rise of the biographical genre has popularized a very specific form of life-writing built upon a pact; a contract of trust signed by narrators and readers. This biographical understanding of life-writing has overshadowed other forms of bonding with words in which the individual self is not the ultimate destination. Biographies, thus, are a recent invention. Even though writing life, writing about life, and writing biographies may now seem one and the same, they are not. *Bios*—life—and *graphia*—writing—are not limited to a self-affirmative homodiegetic narration of an individual's personality.

Saint Augustine of Hippo (AD 354–430) wrote two very different books of lives, the *Confessions* and the *Rule*. Those books tell a different story of the self. They tell the story of a self that inhabits this passing time of ours until it learns to see beyond its own skin. By reading these two books together, we learn that the monastic life chosen by Augustine in AD 386 was the fruit of a meticulously meditated plan to overcome human chronology—the temporality of the Fall—in an attempt to join God's absolute eternity. The self of the *Confessions* is not the protagonist of an autobiography; instead, the self is a ladder to be thrown away as soon as it takes us to our destination. Since that destination, wholly inhabiting God's eternal love, is ultimately unreachable for as long as we stay alive, Augustine's *Rule* emerges as a mirror conceived to guide us to the mystical city of New Jerusalem. The gates of New Jerusalem will only open after the death of death itself and only those whose names are written in the Book of Life will enter. To aid in that journey, Augustine's *Rule* bestows upon us a map of Christian imitation. A mirror that tells the story of a human life attempting to recreate the unblemished koinon—the shared life—described in Acts of the Apostles 4:32–35. Despite the great heights of goodness and love reached in the *Rule*'s pages, its content is not what matters most; at the end of the day, its precepts merely describe a house of love governed by the shared principles of the Tablets of the Law and Christ's own Sermon on the Mount. The secret inside of the *Rule* is the fact that imitation—a very particular following of the rule—is hinted as the ultimate key to the holy city of New Jerusalem.

Content

Self-Inscription

What is the purpose of writing life? Saint Augustine believes that we must write life by reading—imitating—the holy life of Christ and the apostles. As members of the Body of Christ, a body politic based on community as communion, Christians are expected to transcend the writing of their individual lives. No individual narration is complete without the Body. To assist in the journey of humanity comprising the universal biography, Augustine writes a manual on how to share our lives: "The chief motivation for your sharing life together is to live harmoniously in the house and to have one heart and one soul seeking God" (*Praeceptum* I.2–3).[1] Known for his innovative writing of his own life in the *Confessions*, Augustine's greatest contribution to the realm of biographical literature is in fact his courage in crafting a universal biography of mankind in the *Rule*. Before the invention of writing, however, life was

---

[1]Augustine's choice of words is very deliberate: "Primum, propter quod in unum estis congregati ut unianimes habitetis in domo et sit uobis anima una et cor unum in deum" (*Praeceptum* I.2–3). His relationship with words is explained by himself within the context of the early Christian debates on classical rhetoric and the compatibility of the Gospel and the literary devices of antiquity. Socrates and Plato had questioned the subservience of message to ornament in the context of the Sophistic tradition; similarly, third-century Christians questioned the need to rely on ornament and rhetoric when communicating the lowly, universal message of the Gospels. Saint Augustine's *On Christian Teaching* helped pacify the disputation by arguing that Christians could and should take serene advantage of the artistic tools at their disposal as long as the ornament of words served the Word but not the other way around. His training in classical education shines across his works. Moreover, as George Lawless has pointed out to explain his careful translation, the *Rule* is a text with a distinct "urging that it be read publicly once a week. For this reason, special care has been taken to preserve much of its parallel and antithetical structure along with many of its sonorous qualities" (*Augustine of Hippo and His Monastic Rule*, "Preface" x).

inscribed. Parietal art is the act of engraving life; petroglyphs, the physical inscription of the self on the rocky bed of our planet, are possibly the most fundamental form of biography. A hand exerting mild force telling the world: I carve, therefore I am.[2] First-person writing, possibly a fiction altogether, poses the question: What does it mean to inscribe a life? Since you are reading a book about the text of existence, an expeditious genealogy of life-writing can help elucidate the concept.

The oldest of known laws began with Babylonian king Hammurabi (1810–1750 BC) engraving himself in stone and not so humbly declaring, "I am a hero" ("Hammburabi's Laws" 33, P8). A leader entrusted with the defense of the divine-given law before his people; a writer of first-person literature. Ages past Hammurabi's time, Plutarch (AD 46–119) set out to capture the glory of the culture's greats and he did so by establishing the isomorphic nature of forty-some eminent *Parallel Lives* in a book that also challenges our concept of biographical writing. Another paramount first-person legacy from Antiquity saw Marcus Aurelius (AD 121–80) writing a collection of things to himself often translated as *Meditations*. The things he said to himself, too, prove that there are many ways to write a life beyond the parameters of modern biography.

Due to theological developments regarding the concept of the individuality and the person, the Christian worldview that nourished Augustine's thought swiftly became invested in the writing of lives and life. Even in this context, early Christians did not write biographies, but acts, accounts of martyrdom, and hagiographical

---

[2]Following the donation of the Tablets of the Law in Exodus 31 and the subsequent apostasy of the people in favor of the golden calf, God Himself tells Moses that the new covenant will be founded inside a rock: "I who show favor to whom I will, I who grant mercy to whom I will. But you cannot see my face, for no one can see me and live. Here, continued the Lord, is a place near me where you shall station yourself on the rock. When my glory passes I will set you in the cleft of the rock and will cover you with my hand until I have passed by" (Exodus 33:19–21). The Gospels will continue this lineage in Matthew 16:18, "And so I say to you, you are Peter, and upon this rock I will build my church, and the gates of the netherworld shall not prevail against it." Michelangelo Buonarroti (1475–1564) inscribed the Latin version of the famous versicle "Tu es Petrus et super hanc petram aedificabo ecclesiam mean et tibi dabo claves regni caelorum" around the base of the magnificent dome's drum of Saint Peter's Basilica. Identical inscriptions can be found in Philadelphia's Cathedral of Saints Peter and Paul and others around the world.

portraits instead—all of which address life according to vastly different frameworks; etymologically, martyrdom is a form of testimony, among which shines the early passion of Saints Perpetua and Felicity authored in year 203 by Carthaginian martyr Vibia Perpetua (AD 182–203).[3] Along those lines, our very own Saint Augustine of Hippo, perhaps the inventor of interiority as we know it, legated several books that greatly advanced life-writing as a family of genres. Thirteen books of *Confessions* where the history of the self gives way to the theology of Creation; a chronicle of the struggling soul in the form of his beautiful *Soliloquies*; a monastic *Rule* that serves as a handbook for the good life; and, toward the end of his life, an assortment of retractations or retreatises, *Retractations* that manifest Augustine's self-reflectiveness in the realm of life-writing.

Augustine's Lives

Saint Augustine of Hippo is the author of both one of the earliest self-introspections ever composed and the first monastic rule in the Western world. These two texts may seem disparate in their purpose, but both of them advanced the idea of life-writing in profound ways. The present book explains why Augustine first needed to compose a life-in-time in the form of the *Confessions'* nine opening books so that he could then, only then, create a life-in-eternity in the collection of monastic rules known as *Regula Sancti Augustini*.

---

[3]Alban Butler's tome, *Lives of the Saints*, includes a note referring to Augustine's knowledge and reaction to the veneration of the famous martyrs: "The record of the passion of St Perpetua, St Felicity and their companions is one of the greatest hagiological treasures that have come down to us. In the fourth century these acts were publicly read in the churches of Africa, and were in fact so highly esteemed that St Augustine found it necessary to issue a protest against their being place on a level with the Holy Scriptures" (*Lives of the Saints I*, VI.493). The act of witness is culminated by the rite of peace at the end of "SS. Perpetua, Felicity and their Companions, Martyrs (AD 203)": "the fickle people were clamouring for them to come out into the open, which they did willingly, and after giving each other the kiss of peace, they were killed by the gladiators, Perpetua guiding to her own throat the sword of her nervous executioner, who had failed to kill her at the first stroke, so that she shrieked out with pain. 'Perhaps so great a woman. Could not else have been slain except she willed it'" (*Lives of the Saints I*, VI.498).

Even though Books I–IX follow the archetypical chronological format, reading the *Confessions* as an autobiography is an exercise that obscures the capital difference between modern and premodern life literature. Composed during the last three years of the fourth century, the *Confessions* are not a narration trying to establish a pact between Augustine and the readers, but a confession in the technical sense: a profession of faith.[4] Ultimately, Augustine does not seek to understand or justify his own self. Not even in the chronological, retrospective portion of the book. He does not absolve the history of his personality, either. Against the modern autobiographical pact, the saint from Thagaste does not ask readers to trust him. On the contrary, he uses them as a ladder. A desultory ladder—Wittgenstein's (*Tractatus Logico-Philosophicus* §6.54) or Jacob's (Genesis 28:12)?—that he will gladly disown once he reaches the center of the confession.[5]

---

[4]The distinction between a revelation of what was occult, and a profession of faith can be found in an influential article by Joseph Ratzinger, later Benedict XVI, demonstrating the autonomy of the early Christian concept of confession amidst the ancient world ("Originalität und Überlieferung in Augustins Begriff der *confessio*").
[5]Perpetua had a similar vision: "I beheld a ladder of bronze, marvelously great, reaching up to heaven; and it was narrow, so that not more than one might go up at one time. And in the sides of the ladder were planted all manner of things of iron. There were swords there, spears, hooks, and knives; so that if any that went up took not good heed or looked not upward, he would be torn and his flesh cling to the iron. And there was right at the ladder's foot a serpent lying, marvelously great, which lay in wait for those that would go up, and frightened them that they might not go up. Now Saturus went up first (who afterwards had of his own free will given up himself for our-sakes, because it was he who had edified us; and when we were taken he had not been there). And he came to the ladder's head; and he turned and said: Perpetua, I await you; but see that serpent bite you not. And I said: it shall not hurt me, in the name of Jesus Christ. And from beneath the ladder, as though it feared me, it softly put forth its head; and as though I trod on the first step I trod on its head. And I went up, and I saw a very great space of garden, and in the midst a man sitting, white-headed, in shepherd's clothing, tall milking his sheep; and standing around in white were many thousands. And he raised his head and beheld me and said to me: Welcome, child. And he cried to me, and from the curd he had from the milk he gave me as it were a morsel; and I took it with joined hands and ate it up; and all that stood around said, Amen. And at the sound of that word I awoke, yet eating I know not what of sweet. And at once I told my brother, and we knew it should be a passion; and we began to have no hope any longer in this world" (*The Passion of Saints Perpetua and Felicity* 4).

Books I–IX cover the first thirty-three years of Augustine's life in a fairly chronological manner culminating in the turning point of his conversion in AD 386; let us not forget that the conversion is too the beginning of his monastic commitment, for there is no converted Augustine without monk Augustine. Book X, the chapter where the self is questioned—and probably refuted—serves as a fulcrum and aligns with Augustine, the author, as he is writing the *Confessions* between AD 397 and 400. The three remaining books, XI–XIII, transcend human chronology and venture into one of history's deepest reflections on the nature and role of time. Chronology, present questioning, and eternity. It is crucial to note that these phases of Augustine's seemingly autobiographical writing elide the portion of the author's life that most often champions modern autobiographies: the end-product of the Bildungsroman, that is, the mature—flaws and vices included—homodiegetic narrator which seeks to justify the preceding journey of choices. As soon as there is conversion, there is no Augustine—the narrator. Augustine—the author—is born again and all the first things have passed for him. Chronology, the time of humans, is no longer his horizon. He knows he will have to persevere within the boundaries of finitude, but the self-centeredness of mortal chronology is now seen as a mountain to climb. The *Soliloquies* are Augustine's chronicle on the history of a soul's struggle. The *Rule* is his handbook on how to come out victorious in that struggle, with help of sisters, brothers, and God.

In the Augustinian world of life-writing, the self is a necessary toll, a rite of passage; never the protagonist of a biography such as the texts we consume today. "Mihi quaestio factus sum" (*Confessions* X.33.50), I have made myself question, sets the origin of all Augustinian inquiry. The saint's first-person writing is defined by the refutation of the myths of self-transparency and self-causation, a self-questioning gesture that vividly predates the hermeneutics of suspicion. When Jean-Jacques Rousseau (1712–78), author of the archetypical modern autobiography, publishes *Les confessions*, something changes deep inside the act of life-writing. Before the 1760s, writing lives and biographing remained considerably different endeavors. Diametrically opposed to the foundation of the modern essay upon doubt by Michel de Montaigne (1533–92), Rousseau avers to know himself "intus et in cute," as the book's frontispiece reads (*Confessions*, "Préambule"). A spearhead of the evolution of modern sensibilities after Montaigne, Rousseau is everything but doubt. As a necessary consequence of the new paradigm, his book speaks exclusively about himself.

According to Philippe Lejeune's seminal work from 1975, *Le pacte autobiographique*, the new paradigm of life-writing is one where authors and readers sign a pact of textual trust based on the credibility of the individual holding the pen. Autobiographical writing—by definition a modern literary genre—is characterized as a "Recit retrospectif en prose qu'une personne reel/e fait de sa propre existence, lorsqu'el/e met l'accent sur sa vie individuelle, en particulier sur l'histoire de sa personnalite" (14). On the other hand, Augustine's *Confessions* embody a dramatically opposed archetype of first-person writing. Contrary to the self-discovering-the-self, Saint Augustine's semblance of biography is marked by its fierce self-questioning-the-self. Mercifully, the end of the illusion of self-sufficiency is not the end of all things. According to Augustine, this is in fact the only proper beginning: the acknowledgment—a confession—that the only reason why he ever knew anything was because he found something—someone—other than himself inside his own self. Rousseau triumphantly proclaims having conquered knowledge of his interiority and skin; Augustine cuts his heart open for us to see it right before he is born again as a Christian. As he struggles to accept that the self is not the last frontier, he battles against his old self and seeks solace. Luckily, he found the place and way to do it.

Between the summer and fall of AD 386, Augustine joined friends and relatives in the georgic estate of Cassiciacum. A period of intellectual and social flourish, leaving Milan symbolizes the saint's first attempt at coenobitic living. While partaking in this propaedeutic monastic life with a cohort of like-minded companions, Augustine and his colleagues shared quarters, nature, and philocalia. The readings and conversations, however, seem to stir more unrest than the peace for which he had been hoping. The garden of Cassiciacum is not the hortus conclusus of the Marian tradition, but an open orchard—hortus apertus?—where the self is not enclosed but burst open as Augustine breaks his formerly self-imposed restraints. The little garden of Cassiciacum thus became the battlefield for "the burning struggle which I had entered upon against myself; to what solution, Thou didst know, but I did not. Yet, my madness was healthful and my dying was life-giving; I was aware of the extent of my evil, but I was unaware of the extent of the good I would shortly attain" (*Confessions* VIII.8.19). Augustine writes from the self and about the self because he has come to the realization that there is nothing else he can do. The first person is the only means for him to prove that himself—his self—is, indeed, not his own. Augustine's confession is not a self-centered exposé of his ego, but a genealogy of the impropriety of the self and a gateway to finding mankind's true center.

Nonetheless, there is a chronology to Books I–X of the *Confessions*. There is a discourse in its essential, fluvial sense of flowing current. Then, time is sublated. Book X evinces the transition from the temporality of humans to the time of God. Chronology, the time of fallen mortals, ceases as the theological portion of the book gives way to the temporality of eternity. The trance of Augustine's conversion and the subsequent path toward the divine, however, does not end with the *Confessions*. Often neglected, the *Rule* is the other great book about a human life written by Saint Augustine. The *Confessions* tell the story of the saint's life in time. The *Rule* tells the story of how to turn time into eternity while we are still alive. A history of times to come that is not an indicative, but imperative narration. To overcome the barriers of temporality, we need to recreate a nonchronological type of existence. A monastic rule is an active simulation or imitation, then a brotherly production of a shared time that is meaningful; a sense of temporality that is both inside and outside human chronology. If we want to trace Augustine's monastic steps, we need to learn how to follow a rule.

2

Thy Name Is Written

Born in Language

Language is the house of life and Saint Augustine does not hesitate to stipulate how the quality of our existential writing can be appraised: "Here again, you will know the extent of your progress as you enlarge your concern for the common interest instead of your own private interest; enduring love will govern all matters pertaining to the fleeting necessities of life" (*Praeceptum* V.2).[1] Yet, how do we appraise Augustine's own appraisal? How can we establish whether his interpretation of the role and nature of imitation—writing our life by living it according to the holy paragon—is not just desirable, but optimal? To do so, we need to examine the meaning of language in Augustine's rule-writing.

Augustine and Wittgenstein scholar, Miles Hollingworth, has not only written the two most-insightful books on Augustine but also the most thought-provoking book on the Austrian philosopher to come out since Saul Kripke's *Wittgenstein on Rules and Private Language*. Whereas many interpreters keep reading the lives of Augustine and Wittgenstein without questioning the hermeneutical axioms found in our modern concept of biography, Hollingworth's corpus advances a total theory of life-writing which demands the text of the Augustinian *Rule* to be reconsidered as a backward script writing.

---

[1]"Et ideo, quanto amplius rem communem quam propria uestra curaueritis, tanto uos amplius profecisse noueritis; ut in omnibus quibus utitur transitura necessitas, superimineat, quae permanet, caritas" (*Praeceptum* V.2).

As he captures a fundamental move at the heart of Wittgenstein's wager, Hollingworth's *Ludwig Wittgenstein* is the book that proves that the ordinary language turn is in fact an ordinary life turn. Likewise, Augustine's coenobitic rule is the script of a pilgrimage to heaven which is composed of the tools of ordinary life—coexistence, forgiveness, clothing, nourishment, labor. In the case of Wittgenstein, his final works contributed to legitimizing academic speech about ordinary language and use. As such, the linguistic turn originally deployed in the realm of formal logic as the structure or possibility of language—*Tractatus Logico-Philosophicus*—was populated not just by artificial languages, but also by the consuetudinary acts of everyday meaning—*Philosophical Investigations*. Hollingworth's theory of life-writing defies the very meaning of biography in a different way than premodern life-writing did. Whereas the latter simply did not operate under the parameters of a subject like ours, the former exploits the cracks of the modern subject embodied by Ludwig Wittgenstein the human. Ultimately, we unearth a biography about the failure of Wittgenstein's modern subject and the philosopher's bold awareness of this fact. By conquering this vantage point, *Ludwig Wittgenstein* allows us to perceive the backward theory of life embraced by Wittgenstein. One that, maybe not too surprisingly, astonishingly resembles the backward theory of life as written in Augustine's *Rule* of imitation. "Act like your Biography," this provocation by Hollingworth captivatingly captures Wittgenstein's understanding of the life-language isomorphism. By challenging the very possibility of meaning through the rule-following paradox, Wittgenstein also demands that we revise our theory of life. And, who is the author of Augustine's biography? The only one who he cared to imitate in the *Rule*, that is, Christ Himself. How did Wittgenstein and Augustine's concept of backward enacting of the existential script become so entangled?

At some point between 1936 and 1946, Ludwig Wittgenstein (1889–1951) wrote a series of notes that would only be posthumously published under the title *Philosophical Investigations*. This series of drafts is responsible for the development of one of the greatest philosophical debates in recent history. Wittgenstein's rule-following paradox—the possibility that rules and words may not mean anything at all—showed that rules—even monastic rules?—were a problem of language. Unwary readers, at least those who had not previously reached the final pages of the *Tractatus Logico-Philosophicus*, could perhaps be surprised by the fact that Wittgenstein is not the first one to speak in that posthumous treatise. Saint Augustine of Hippo is. It is in Augustine's *Confessions* where Wittgenstein finds the theory of language and life that allows him to unfold his critique and, maybe, a solution to the ultimate problem of language and meaning. To the very problem of life.

In the 1930s and 1940s, Ludwig Wittgenstein exposed a sort of Crypto-Augustinism in the fact that he found a theory of language in Augustine's semblance of autobiography when the Austrian philosopher decided to speak again after having thrown away the ladder in the *Tractatus Logico-Philosophicus*'s memorable Proposition 6.54. The silence ensuing Proposition 7 was finally broken in the form of a major work, *Philosophical Investigations*. A timeless treatise to break the self-imposed silence. First words anew coming, however, from the unexpected voice of Augustine's *Confessions*. Unknowingly or not, Wittgenstein's Augustinian remarks set in motion one of the most fervent intellectual debates of the twentieth century: The rule and private language argument. Reactions erupted as many contemporary thinkers questioned the very nature of our language and lives. Wittgenstein's rule-following paradox can be solved by looking at the full meaning of the word in contention, as much as the rules of language in Augustine can only be understood if we pay close attention to the monastic rule of life written by the saint from Thagaste. To obey a rule is to imitate a rule.

After the mystical closure of *Tractatus Logico-Philosophicus*'s Proposition 7, the Wittgenstein of the *Philosophical Investigations* became concerned with the language of life. He became captivated by everything which can still be said after having thrown away the ladder. Contrary to the original intuition of propositional logic, the realm before scientific propositions and true philosophy, that is, the realm of ordinary language might still have something to say. Unable to begin speaking on his own, for his self-imposed silence was strong, Wittgenstein asks Augustine for help on his quest for the essence of language. To do so, Wittgenstein delegates the honor of opening the new book as he transcribes an episode from *Confessions* I.8.13 where Augustine recalls the very moment in which he became a boy. According to the saint's retrospective introspection, language marks the passage from infancy toward boyhood. When Wittgenstein lets

Augustine speak, he is letting mature Augustine speak about the discovery of language by young Augustine. It is worth having a look at the exact fragment encapsulated by Wittgenstein:

> When they (my elders) named some object, and accordingly moved towards something, I saw this and I grasped that the thing was called by the sound they uttered when they meant to point it out. Their intention was shewn by their bodily movements, as it were the natural language of all peoples: the expression of the face, the play of the eyes, the movement of other parts of the body, and the tone of voice which expresses our state of mind in seeking, having, rejecting, or avoiding something. Thus, as I heard words repeatedly used in their proper places in various sentences, I gradually learnt to understand what objects they signified; and after I had trained my mouth to form these signs, I used them to express my own desires. (*Philosophical Investigations* §I; *Confessions* I.8.13)

Wittgenstein selects these Augustinian words because they "give us a particular picture of the essence of human language" (*Philosophical Investigations* §i). There is something else. While the *Philosophical Investigations* resume Wittgenstein's more geometric methodology and appear numbered despite being themselves a collection of notes and remarks, the book is lacking the first article, strictly speaking. Articles 2–693 are numbered using Arabic numerals. Part II is numbered using roman numerals. In Part I, the first article stands as a solitary "i," with section §1 actually being Wittgenstein's Augustinian glosses and marginalia. Will we be surprised when we realize that this part characterizes a language that can never really be our own? Not only are the *Philosophical Investigations* a book about someone else's linguistic turn, but they also contain something that goes past mere academic citation. The opening section of Wittgenstein's book is someone else's book. More than just witty wordplay, this constitutes an essential philosophical clue. Augustine's theory of life expressed in the *Rule* points at the exact same phenomenon: as much as our words are never really ours, our true life is exactly what we cannot call our own.

The picture of language which Wittgenstein unearths in the works of Augustine is a familiar one. Language as ostension. The interplay of language and body as we indicate, signal, and connect meanings. The resulting, realist theory of language in Augustine is one where an almost structuralist mesh of meanings covers all of reality. A system where "Every word has a meaning. This meaning is correlated with the word. It is the object for which the word stands" (§i). What is the source of meaning? What happens when we say and do? Why do we infer meaning from words, instructions, and sentences? Therefrom, Wittgenstein goes on to argue that this is just one among a number of conceivable systems of language. We will come back to it soon enough, but first, it is urgent to revise what Wittgenstein left out of his Augustinian vignette.

The fragment selected by Wittgenstein serves as a picturesque introduction to the ostensive theory of language. In the late 1930s and early 1940s, Wittgenstein was indeed concentrating on the nature of language. Its essence, he said. But Augustine's full chapter yields a much deeper picture of language than the one divulged in this selective quotation. The use of language by young Augustine in the fragment quoted by Wittgenstein is indeed ostensive, but the sentences leading to and immediately following his citation stress everything that is at stake for Augustine's mature self as he recounts his own linguistic turn. As the *Philosophical Investigations* are supposed to depart from the simple ostensive understanding of language as a first propaedeutic maneuver into alternative, more complex types of language, the whole book unwarily becomes a commentary on how somebody else became a fully linguistic being, which is what Augustine is really talking about in the chronological portion of the *Confessions*. That is exactly what Wittgenstein's gloss chooses to omit:

Is it not true that, advancing from infancy toward the present, I came to boyhood? Or did it come into me, succeeding infancy? The latter did not go away; where, indeed, could it go? Nevertheless, it did not now exist. For, I was not an infant (one who could not speak), but was now a boy able to talk. This I do remember, and I observed afterwards how I learned to speak. The older people did not teach me by suggesting the words to me according to any definite method of instruction, as was the case a little later with the alphabet; rather, with my own mind which Thou gavest me, O Lord, I wished to make known with divers grunts and sounds and with divers gestures the meanings within my heart, so that my will would be obeyed. (*Confessions* I.8.13)

Language is the second birth of the person. The one through which the young join the world. Predating the Heideggerian being-in-the-world, language is Augustine's rite of passage too. One, like Heidegger's, that is neither objective nor subjective, neither endogenous nor exogenous—did Augustine come to boyhood or did it come to him? Not unlike Heidegger, the saint is just thrown into being-there; as an infant, "one who could not speak," Augustine's process of acquiring the ability to speak is what makes him be in the world. If language throws Augustine into the world of humans, what or who is this language that is throwing Augustine? We could argue about the theological foundations of Heidegger's thought and the role of the mystical in Wittgenstein, but while those realms are deliberately left in a haze of mystery, Saint Augustine does not hesitate for a second: God is the one who put meaning in his heart. He also gifted the tools for young Augustine to unveil and begin using those inner meanings.

Remembering the coming of age through language would require Augustine to remember the prelinguistic phase of his childhood. This challenges a few hundred theories of language acquisition and cognitive development. So be it. Regardless of what we may think, old Augustine is perfectly aware of how—human—language is acquired. Ostension, repetition, correction, and quite a bit of whipping by adults who seem to have forgotten that they were also children once. The alphabet, Augustine says, he acquired this way. The divine gift of the mind allows him to harness words and, as a consequence, become more and more capable of concurrently harnessing his will. Luckily, the language of the human tongue is only part of the story.

Dead-End of Philosophy

Wittgenstein's *Tractatus* is a demonstration of the linguistic nature of our philosophical problems. Our loose, off-limits use of language is caused by an illusion of confidence. The problem is that the language needed to solve the issue of what might legitimately be said is not really a human language. On the other hand, a human language is unlikely to overcome the obstacles at the limits of philosophical saying. As Wittgenstein points out:

> Here it is easy to get into that dead-end in philosophy, where one believes that the difficulty of the task consists in our having to describe phenomena that are hard to get hold of, the present experience that slips quickly by, or something of the kind. Where we find ordinary language too crude, and it looks as if we were having to do, not with the phenomena of every-day, but with ones that "easily elude us, and, in their coming to be and passing away, produce those others as an average effect." (Augustine: Manifestissima et usitatissima sunt, et eadem rusus nimis latent, et nova est inventio eorum.) (*Philosophical Investigations* §436)

A skeptical reading of Wittgenstein will have to concede that nothing coming out of a human, ordinary, crude language can claim to hold any kind of truth value. A late-Wittgensteinian approach, however, will conclude that this realization should not prevent us from aspiring to achieve decent levels of truth as a serene and honest convention. As expected, Augustine's reliance on God as the only source of truth solves the dead-end of philosophy by positing the existence of an altogether different language underlying all languages, including all human language games and even all of the logic itself. Wittgenstein identifies, yet fails to name, this deep axiom of Augustine's worldview when he notes,

> Augustine describes the learning of human language as if the child came into a strange country and did not understand the language of the country; that is, as if it already had a language, only not this one. Or again: as if the child could already *think* only not yet speak. And "think" would here mean something like "talk to itself." (*Philosophical Investigations* §32)

Wittgenstein cannot see that having another language and talking to itself are two realizations of impossibility whose impossibility is pulverized by the fact that Augustine's Ursprache—a language before language—is not another human code.

The ostensive picture of language left by Wittgenstein's pruning had only told half the story, for that one was the language of the "stormy society of human life"; the very language and society of the Fall that Augustine's monastic adventure was hoping to sublate. Exactly at the stage of the *Confessions* where Wittgenstein halted his quotation of Augustine, the saint recalls acquiring another language. While the language of the earthly city is a necessary evil, Saint Augustine is mostly concerned exactly with the code that Wittgenstein omitted: God's Word and the traces of it still found in human language. The good news is that we can discover it just by continuing to read the *Confessions* immediately subsequent chapter: "As a boy, I began to pray to Thee, my Help and my Refuge, and by invoking Thee I broke the knots which bound my tongue" (*Confessions* I.9.14). The dead-end of philosophy—the knots of the tongue—is cut by a nonhuman language present in all humans. The Verbum ruling all verbs structure the possibilities of language, but it is not the empty, purely structural system embodied by the *Tractatus*'s concept of logic. Logic must be devoid of content, for "The propositions of logic describe the scaffolding of the world, or rather they represent it. They have no 'subject-matter'" (*Tractatus* §6.124). As a system of possibilities that renders everything that is conceivable, Augustine's logic is no less structural than that of Wittgenstein; the former does have a structural nature as the Book of Creation or the Book of Nature but, unlike Wittgenstein's, it also contains one proposition that transcends logic: the Love of God. All logical possibilities are made possible by the simple, incommensurable fact that God decides to create His laws and world. Augustine will call interpretation the process of finding this divine love in all the propositions of the world and all the propositions of logic itself. Convinced that there is a divine language underneath every potential human language and action, Augustine provides a manual—a rule—for reading the text of nature. The verbal condition of existence does not, however, mean that we should just sit back and wait for our life's plot to be read to us by someone else. In the world of Augustine, a divine syntax exists but the content of each one of our script's lines is yet to be realized and it is the individual's duty to embrace this subsidiary scriptural task. By looking at the textual foundation of humanity, Augustine's *Rule* presents its own integrated solution to the problem of private language, rule-following, meaning, and freedom. This is the safest path to understanding the meaning of the Book of Life.

On Following a Rule

Philosophical Investigations §31 involves Wittgenstein imagining a game of chess. How is chess learned? A likely path sees our learner ostensively grasping basic languages and acquiring rules by intuitively observing the governing concepts and principles. A major question arises, what does it really mean to understand and follow a rule? A rule is the opposite of an occurrence; an accident:

> It is not possible that there should have been only one occasion on which someone obeyed a rule [. . .] To obey a rule, to make a report, to give an order, to play a game of chess, are customs (uses, institutions). To understand a sentence means to understand a language. To understand a language means to be master of a technique. (*Philosophical Investigations* §201–2)

Haphazardly moving a piece of wood roughly shaped like a queen is not playing chess. A seasoned chess player could perhaps recognize some of these random gesticulations as resembling the legal move of one of his favorite game's pieces. But would the person moving the pieces really be playing chess? Does that person need to intend to play chess in order to play chess? And, could I come up with a completely different, secret system of rules that would make up my own universe? Would that be a game? If everything—any random move or meaning—can be subsumed under a rule, does the rule mean anything at all? Wittgenstein explores this conundrum in one of the most influential fragments of the twentieth century:

> This was our paradox: no course of action could be determined by a rule, because every course of action can be made out to accord with the rule. The answer was: if everything can be made out to accord with the rule, then it can also be made out to conflict with it. And so there would be neither accord nor conflict here [. . .] What this shews is that there is a way of grasping a rule which is not an interpretation, but which is exhibited in what we call "obeying the rule" and "going against it" in actual cases. Hence there is an inclination to say: every action according to the rule is an interpretation. But we ought to restrict the term

"interpretation" to the substitution of one expression of the rule for another. (*Philosophical Investigations* §201)

This realization has transformational consequences in so far as meaning goes. Is meaning anything more than a somewhat reproducible mirage? After all, a repeatable illusion may be all we need. Wittgenstein himself was always more interested in the existential and even mystical dimensions of life than what most of his interpreters gathered by looking at the apparent dryness of the *Tractatus* and the informal tone of the *Philosophical Investigations*. He was indeed concerned with math, logic, and language. But that is not something contrary to life. That meaning might be related to obeying or following a rule, and vice versa, which has extremely powerful implications because, as Wittgenstein propounds, "'obeying a rule' is a practice. And to think one is obeying a rule is not to obey a rule. Hence it is not possible to obey a rule 'privately': otherwise thinking one was obeying a rule would be the same thing as obeying it" (*Philosophical Investigations* §202).[2] This changes everything. I can play pretend at home or in the woods and call myself a chess player, a philosopher, or a monk. If there is no practice supporting those words, they ring hollow and perish. I can even create my own language game and call myself a *nonk. A *nonk living a *nonkish life worshipping false idol *Nonk, perhaps. My

---

[2]Many valuable studies on the problems of rule-following and private language have been written in the last few decades, starting with the seminal book by Saul Kripke, *Wittgenstein on Rules and Private Language*. Many intelligent chapters can be found in the collective works coordinated by Alexpander Miller and Crispin Wright, *Rule-Following and Meaning*, as well as Christopher M. Leich and Steven H. Holtzman, *Wittgenstein: To Follow a Rule*. Leich and Holtzman's opening text is entitled "Introductory Essay: Communal Agreement and Objectivity" and it provides a serene summary of Wittgenstein's increasing mistrust on the self: "To begin with, we should notice that Wittgenstein's commitment to that constitutive claim must involve him in rejecting the thought that one has a *privileged* access to one's own understanding of a word, an access that does not rely on observation of one's own applications of the word, and is indeed more dependable than the access afforded by such observation [. . .] Now it is well known that Wittgenstein does indeed mount an attack against this notion of privileged access, and indeed that the dismissal of the claim to objectivity in §258 plays a crucial role in it" (9). In a later article, Wittgenstein explicitly questions the referentiality of the self: "there is a great variety of criteria for personal 'identity.' Now which of them determines my saying that '*I*' am in pain? None" (*Philosophical Investigations* §404).

fraudulent life means nothing because there is no practice. There
can be no practice if I am alone in my *nonky world of *nonkness.
For languages, rules, and practices to mean something, we need at
least someone else with whom the rule, maybe our illusory world,
is shared.[3] That would not make it reasonable or less ridiculous,
but it is the least we need for something to mean something. This
powerful move renders Wittgenstein both an unexpected critic
of hollow individuality and a surprising theoretical provider for
contemporary monastic theory. First, Wittgenstein offers a renewed
take on the red line of self-questioning that ties medieval thought to
the nineteenth-century hermeneutics of suspicion:

> There is no such thing as the subject that thinks or entertains
> ideas. If I wrote a book called *The World as I found it*, I should
> have to include a report on my body, and should have to say
> which parts were subordinate to my will, and which were not,
> etc., this being a method of isolating the subject, or rather of
> showing that in an important sense there is no subject; for it
> alone could not be mentioned in that book. (*Tractatus* §5.631)

Wittgenstein is well aware of the Humean-Kantian problem of
causation and its consequences in the realm of human subjectivity.
If the idea of causation is but a useful fiction that we erect in

---

[3]Wittgenstein goes as far as talking about self-discipline. Interestingly, experts
such as Verheijen and Van Bavel have corroborated extensively that Augustine's
monasticism is a particularly laconic one in regards to asceticism. Loving God and
neighbor, the shared language game, seems to him like a more profitable enterprise
because there can be hollow asceticism: "A human being can encourage himself, give
himself orders, obey, blame and punish himself; he can ask himself a question and
answer it. We could even imagine human beings who spoke only in monologue; who
accompanied their activities by talking to themselves. An explorer who watched
them and listened to their talk might succeed in translating their language into ours.
(This would enable him to predict these people's actions correctly, for he also hears
them making resolutions and decisions.) But could we also imagine a language in
which a person could write down or give vocal expression to his inner experiences—
his feelings, moods, and the rest—for his private use?—Well, can't we do so in
our ordinary language?–But that is not what I mean. The individual words of this
language are to refer to what can only be known to the person speaking; to his
immediate private sensations. So another person cannot understand the language"
(*Philosophical Investigations* §243).

order to make sense of experience's otherwise discombobulated individual perceptions, the notion of a continuing, unified, and unifying human self crumbles before our very eyes. As far as the *Tractatus* goes, Wittgenstein cannot seem to acquiesce to the Kantian *Prolegomena*'s attempt to overcome—or maybe just distract us from—Hume's ferocious, but fair criticism of the unity of experience. At the end of the day, can we really say that Kant's necessary unification is really necessary? Without something like Augustine's exogenous causation of soul and body—which they are but warfare while in this life—can we really speak of an empirically deducted unified self that remains constant in time and connects all of our impressions?[4] We can pretend we are something, but private fiction deceives nobody other than myself. That is life. In so far as the negative portion of the argument, Saint Augustine too, as many masters of all ages have done, comes to the same conclusion as Wittgenstein in Book X of the *Confessions*. "Mihi quaestio factus sum" (X.33.50), we have to become questions to ourselves. The self is the test. That is why we are alive. We are born so that we are tempted to praise and worship that which our private impressions tell us to be the center of the universe. The divine test is making us

---

[4] I discussed the problem of identity and the unity of perception at length in the previous volume, *On Hellenism, Judaism, Individualism and Early Christian Theories of the Subject*. Kant's *Prolegomena* provide the optimal point of entry to the discussions on "necessary unification" (§22) and the "synthetic unity of perceptions" (§22). Even though it ultimately resorts to the metaphysical resources he and Hume are trying to overcome, a long, latter section of the treatise addresses Hume's challenge with courage: "In order to make a trial with Hume's problematic concept (his crux metaphysicorum), namely the concept of cause, first, there is given to me a priori, by means of logic, the form of a conditional judgment in general, namely, to use a given cognition as ground and the other as consequent. It is possible, however, that a rule of relation is found in perception which says that a given appearance is constantly followed by another (but not conversely); and this is a case for me to employ the hypothetical judgment and, e.g., to say: if a body is illuminated sufficiently long by the sun, then it becomes warm. Here, there is certainly no necessity of connection as yet, and thus [not] the concept of cause. However, I continue and say that, if the above proposition, which is merely a subjective connection of perceptions, is to be a judgment of experience, then it must be viewed as necessary and universally valid. But such a proposition would be: the sun is through its light the cause of heat. The above empirical rule is now viewed as a law—and, in fact, not as valid merely of appearances, but [valid] of them on behalf of a possible experience, which requires completely and thus necessarily valid rules" (§29).

come to life atop the altar—we started in Paradise, nonetheless—as we are constantly being told by self and the world that we are everything that matters. The fruit is there, hanging low. We have not made ourselves, but we are born to make ourselves question. The chronological, biographical interpretation of the *Confessions* is incompatible with Augustine's words in regards to the causation or self-causation of the subject: "Is anyone going to be the artificer in his own production? Or is there some vein coursing from another source, by which being and life flow into us, other than the fact that Thou makest us, O Lord, to whom being and life are not different things, since the highest Being and the highest Life are identical?" (*Confessions* I.6.10). Therefrom, Augustine says that Jesus knew exactly what He was doing when he condensed the Law into one two-sided principle of saving love: "There is no need to command us to love ourselves and our own bodies, because we love who we are—and also what is below us, yet belongs to us—by an unshakeable law of nature [. . .] It remained only to impose commandments upon us concerning god, who is above us, and our neighbor, who is beside us," such teaching is found in Augustine's formidable *The Teacher* (26).

Jesus does not command self-love. The test of life, the ultimate language game is loving everything else. Wittgenstein realizes that a private language is a worthless illusion of a language because there is no underlying subject. Not one we can trust, that is for sure. On its own, the individual has "no criterion of correctness" (*Philosophical Investigations* §258). It is pointless to talk about the self as a guarantor of meaning because there is no way to collate the private impressions. Despite the opinion of a great portion of the seventeenth- to nineteenth-century philosophers, the self is self-opaque. The monastic connection shines radiantly when we realize that Augustine's mistrust on the self-found in *Confessions* X.27.28—"Thou wert within and I was without"—is the keystone of his communitarian endeavor.[5] The greatest early argument for monastic coenobitism comes from Saint Basil the Great (AD 330–

---

[5] A most peculiar guarantor is postulated in *Philosophical Investigations* §234: "Would it not be possible for us, however, to calculate as we actually do (all agreeing, and so on), and still at every step to have a feeling of being guided by the rules as by a spell, feeling astonishment at the fact that we agreed? (We might give thanks

79), who starkly criticized the risks involved in the solitary nature
of anchoritism, "Community life offers more blessings than can
be fully and easily enumerated" (*Regular Life*, "The Long Rules"
7).[6] A creed of love and service needs someone to love and serve.
Augustine's decisive coenobitic choice supports Basil's argument that
neighbor and God are both needed for us to imitate what Christ did
on the Mount of Beatitudes. Finally, Wittgenstein enquires: "Are the
rules of the private language impressions of rules?—The balance on
which impressions are weighed is not the impression of a balance"
(*Philosophical Investigations* §259). A proper rule needs to be built
on a language that is more than private.

Universal, not Private, Language

Wittgenstein warns us against the risks of relying on the self's auto-
opaque rules and meanings. To amend the ruptured linguistic Babylon
caused by our prideful transgression squandered in the Garden of
Eden, Augustine's resolves to rely on God's universal language. His
rule's propositions are *proposita*, a monastic concept that means
both the intention to live a life and the life itself. This master key

---

to the Deity for our agreement.) This merely shews what goes 'obeying a rule' in
everyday life."

[6] A religion of forgiveness and love—a love that should transcend the Lacanian
sense of instrumental solipsism—cannot exist in a world with just one subject.
Proper anchoritism, as explained by Augustine in his renowned etymology of the
monakhos, is at least a matter of God and self; if possible, though, the presence
of neighbors renders imitating Christ's command of brotherly love a more feasible
enterprise. St. Basil of Caesarea teaches: "Consider, further, that the Lord by reason
of His excessive love for man was not content with merely teaching the word, but,
so as to transmit us clearly and exactly the example of humility in the perfection
of charity, girded Himself and washed the feet of the disciples (John 13:5). Whom,
therefore, will you wash? To whom will you minister? In comparison with whom
will you be the lowest, if you live alone? [. . .] So it is an arena for the combat, a good
path of progress, continual discipline, and a practicing of the Lord's commandments,
when brethren dwell together in community [. . .] It maintains also the practice
characteristic of the saints, of whom it is recorded in the Acts: 'And all they that
believed were together and had all things in common' (Acts 2:44) and again: 'And
the multitude of believers had but one heart and one soul; neither did anyone say
that aught of the things which he possessed was his own, but all things were in
common unto them'" (*Regular Life*, "The Long Rules" 7).

THY NAME IS WRITTEN

was already present in Wittgenstein's quoting of Augustine: "their bodily gestures (the natural speech of all mankind)" (*Confessions* I.8.13). There is acting of the human body that produces universal meaning.

The *Rule*, a monastic rule, is not a textbook. It is not concerned with the language and meaning of the stormy society of human life. It does not pay lip service to the world. On the contrary, by revealing the universal language at the heart of all human languages, it invites others to follow it. Following a monastic rule is liberating language from its earthly limitations. Verbally speaking, it consists of liberating language from the temptations of a private language. When the monastic rule worries about consuetudinary details such as eating, conduct, human relations, or education, it does so in hopes of showing that by changing our conduct we can transform our meaning. Like Augustine's first prayers as a kid, following the monastic rule breaks "the knots which bound my tongue" (*Confessions* I.9.14). It frees language from the self-imposed limitations derived from the squandering of the original freedom, knowledge, and meaning through the Fall. A Fall that had rendered the universal language private.

Wittgenstein quotes Augustine employing the fascinating phrase "the natural speech of all mankind," or, in the Latin original, "verbis naturalibus omnium gentium" (*Confessions* I.8.13). This inner language of the body is not just a figure of speech. Augustine means it. In fact, he constructs an entire genealogy of language that supports that intuition. Before the Fall, Language was one; it is the Fall that shatters and clouds language, effectively unchaining linguistic change and the indefectible proliferation of human languages as we know them. The fact that our ordinary languages prevent us from communicating with our brothers and sisters just because we may have been born in different cities or under different rules is a sign of humanity's fallen nature. It contributes to hiding the fact that we are all equal. That we need each other. All of us.

First, we saw how Wittgenstein skillfully captured the ostensive theory of language in Augustine's *Confessions*. This type of language, however, was just one out of two types of language according to Augustine. The saint is well aware of that distinction. What Wittgenstein calls the Augustinian theory of language is, strictly speaking, the Augustinian theory of fallen language. Human, fallen language in time is made possible by a more powerful language that well transcends ostension and chronological utterance. The divine language of Creation, also known as the Book of Nature—the theory that everything can be interpreted because everything shares the same essential code—and the Book of Life—the participation of human life in that universal code—contained inside the former.

Despite its fallen nature, Augustine does not reject ordinary language. On the contrary, the second book *On Christian Teaching* has him formulate a complete theory of conventional language that long predates the contemporary theories of truth by convention. First, he deploys a basic semiotic theory: "A sign is a thing which, besides the impression that it presents to our senses, causes some other thing to enter our thoughts. For example, at the sight of a footprint, we think of the animal who passed this way and left its track; at the sight of smoke, we recognize that there is a fire beneath it" (*On Christian Teaching* II.1.1). Ostension is here a mental operation from the point of view of a realist metaphysical system. As Wittgenstein noted, words point at things and things point at words. This is the rudimentary—noun-based, for it mostly refers to objects—style of communication captured by Augustine and Wittgenstein. This only gets us so far, but Augustine is, again, well aware of that. Let us have a look at the theory of the fallen, human language before diving into the possibility of a more-than-human language.

Human language after the Fall is one that makes up for its limitations by building interpersonal bridges in form of conventions. Ostension becomes a system of signs that point at a material world that is assumed as real and intelligible. As far as it concerns human beings, "Conventional signs are those which living creatures give to one another" (*On Christian Teaching* II.3). Signs are not perfect, but they are all we have. They establish the possibility of intersubjectivity. As living creatures, we give each other conventional signs.[7] This division implies that there is a series of signs not originated in creatures; a nonconventional set of rules. In the meantime, the

---

[7]Augustine is well aware of multiple layers of mediation, including the presence of human words and humans themselves: "But because words reverberate through the air, then pass away, lasting no longer than the sounds they make, letters were invented as signs of words. Thus voices are presented to the eyes—not in themselves, but through certain unique signs" (*On Christian Teaching* II.4.5), and "Readers, in reading it, seek only to discover the thoughts and will of those who wrote it down and, through them, the will of god, which, we believe, such authors spoke" (II.5.6).

conventional ones are vehicles that "indicate, as far as possible, either the inner movements of their spirit or anything they have sensed or understood. The only reason we have for displaying things by signs is that we may call forth and transfer to another's mind what we who give the sign have in mind" (*On Christian Teaching* II.3). What ensues this characterization of human language is Augustine's fascinating theory of the proliferation of ordinary languages.

Before the Fall, there was one language. The language of Creation; the language of Nature's Book. The Fall set in motion a struggle for linguistic power. Privatization of language.[8] Augustine's

---

[8]Jean-Jacques Rousseau wrote a famous genealogy of inequality entitled *Discourse on the Origin and Foundations of Inequality Among Mankind*. The text is built upon the analysis of the moment when "Right taking place of violence, nature became subject to law; to unfold that chain of amazing events, in consequence of which the strong submitted to serve the weak, and the people to purchase imaginary ease, at the expense of real happiness" (87). Rousseau's selfish-gene-like theory of the bon sauvage is well known: "inequality, almost non-existent among men in the state of nature, derives its force and its growth from the development of our faculties and the progress of the human mind, and at last becomes permanent and lawful by the establishment of property and of laws. It likewise follows that moral inequality, authorized, solely by positive right, clashes with natural right, whenever it is not in proportion to physical inequality; a distinction which sufficiently determines what we are to think of that kind of inequality which obtains in all civilized nations, since it is evidently against the law of nature that children should command old men, and fools lead the wise, and that a handful should gorge themselves with superfluities, while the starving masses lack the barest necessities of life" (138). The contrast between property and possession and the idea of the bon sauvage does not stop there. A most delicate paradox arises when we realize that the exact same appropriation Rousseau denounces in the realm of political philosophy is mimicked by him in that of metaphysics. While Augustine's *Confessions* are a declamation on the impropriety of the self, Rousseau's homonymous treatise departs from a non-demonstrated property of the self by the self. The axiomatic nature of modern individualistic thought is so powerful than even the self-proclaimed paladin of modern communitarianism accepts is unable to see the appropriation at the heart of this theory of the self. From there, all communitarian efforts built on that appropriation will be but a futile suppression of the self-affirmative inclinations of the modern individualistic self. Rousseau's unaware acceptance of the individualistic axiom explains the failure of all modern communitarian efforts. Augustine's *Rule*, on the other hand, aims to build a koinonia of non-appropriated selves conscious of their finitude and convinced that it is in others—mutual service and love in imitation of the Jerusalem koinonia—and the Other that we might find our true self-affirmation. One self-affirmation that, unlike modern communitarianism after Rousseau, does not suppress the other.

take on historical linguistics and biblical paleography is aimed at proving that not only is the universal language possible, but also a factual reality even after the Fall: "divine scripture—which heals such serious diseases of the human will—began from one language" (*On Christian Teaching* II.5.6). The possibility of a common language shared by all of humanity has philological, metaphysical, and theological implications.[9] However, that state would not last

---

[9]The matter of Pentecost is addressed by Augustine in Sermons 227, 228, 257, and 265. "Sermon 227" presents a formidable argumentation in which Augustine cements the idea of unity—harmony, concord, and unanimity—central to the rule through the images of the Lord's Table in which the new covenant returns the multiple to the unity of one original bread and tongue. The main source in this theorization of the body of concord is, again, Acts of the Apostles, the exact archetype where he found the model for the Jerusalem koinonia to be imitated by the monks living according to the *Rule*'s precepts: "I promised you who have just been baptized a sermon to explain the sacrament of the Lord's table, something which you now see and which you were made participants in last night. You need to know what you have received, what you are going to receive, and what you ought to receive daily. That bread, which you see on the altar, sanctified by the Word of God, is the Body of Christ. That cup (or rather what the cup holds), sanctified by the Word of God, is the Blood of Christ. Through these the Lord wished to commemorate for us His Body and Blood, which He poured out for the remission of sins. If you receive them properly, you are what you have received, for the Apostle says: 'we the many are one bread, one body' (1 Cor 10:17). Thus he explained the sacrament of the Lord's table: 'we the many are one bread, one body.' So this bread serves as a reminder to you how much you should love unity. After all, was that bread made up of just one grain? Weren't there many grains of wheat? Before they all came together as bread, they were separate. They were joined together, after a certain amount of pounding, through water. For unless wheat is ground down and sprinkled with water, it can't come together to form what we call bread. In the same way, you too were ground down, so to speak, by the humiliation of fasting and the sacrament of exorcism. Then came baptism, and you were, so to speak, moistened with water so as to form bread. But without fire, it's not bread yet. So what symbolizes the fire? That's the chrism, the oil. That's the sacrament of the Holy spirit, the fueler of the fire" (*Sermons on the Liturgical Seasons* 153, "Sermon 227"). After an indelible, almost ekphrastic description of bread-making as body-making, Augustine exalts the isomorphic nature of bread and the apostolic koinonia after which the church is modeled: "Notice this when the Acts of the Apostles is read. (The reading of the book itself begins soon; today we start the book called 'Acts of the Apostles.') Whoever wants to make progress has a way to do it. When you come together in church, put aside empty talk. Concentrate on the scriptures. We are your books. So pay attention, and you'll see. The Holy spirit will come on Pentecost. And this is how He will come: He will show Himself in tongues of fire. For He breathes charity into us. We are set on fire for God, and we spurn the world, and the straw in us is burned up, and our hearts are, so to speak, refined into

much longer. The universal book, the syntax of the world, bonding all humans as equals were broken when humans decided to erase it by violating the rule of Genesis 2:17:

> Those signs could not be the same for all nations because of the sin of human dissension, when each one sought to seize political control for itself. A sign of this pride is that tower raised up towards heaven where impious humanity merited the just verdict of having not only their minds, but also their voices in dissonant discord (Gn 11:1–9). (*On Christian Teaching* II.2.3)

Vernacular languages and the languages of the world are engendered by pride. Augustine's theology of linguistic change is of course foreign to modern linguistics, but he does not exactly state that linguistic change is corruption per se. Once fallen, linguistic change becomes a natural process. What he says, instead, is that linguistic change does not need to be categorized as decadence or progress unfolding. Even though the price of distancing ourselves from our equals is a high one, dissension is just the new natural after the Fall. The problem is the prideful act that set it all in motion. After the Fall, it is inevitable for the universal language to become more and more fragmented as everyone wants to seize what remains of it. Before economic or social capital, linguistic capital— the control of signs—has been the battlefield where humans have fought for world domination. Language had been a bond uniting all humans as brothers and sisters created in the image and likeness. Unfortunately, due to pride and greed, our words have become instruments of separation, hate, and war. If only there was a way to transform language into a vehicle of love again. Augustine calls that *interpretation*:

> This I do because even the God-given signs found in the Holy scriptures were communicated to us through human beings who wrote them down [. . .] All these signs are, so to speak, visible words [. . .] words have gained by far a preeminence among

---

gold. Therefore, the Holy Spirit draws near, the fire after the water, and you become bread, what is the Body of Christ. That's the way in which unity is symbolized" (154, "Sermon 227").

human beings for expressing whatever ideas in the mind we might want to make public. The Lord, it is true, gave a sign via the perfume of the ointment that His feet were anointed with (Jn 12:3–7); He made known through taste what He intended in the sacrament of His body and blood; and when the woman was healed by touching "the tassel of His cloak" (Mt 9:21), the act signified something. (*On Christian Teaching* II.3)

Words are the selected vehicle for the expression of human ideas, but they are far from the only one. The argument that follows is a prime example of theologically founded linguistics. Because Christ's Body is meaningful, human words are imbued with its perfume; the permeating of all words, Christ's meaning, warrants the reality of deeper meaning; therefore, humans must interpret their own signs and words in order to unveil the underlying truth.[10]

Augustine's theory of the divine perfume gives an account of an otherwise puzzling article found in the *Rule*'s last chapter: "The Lord grant you the grace to observe these precepts with love as lovers of spiritual beauty, exuding the fragrance of Christ in the goodness of your lives; you are no longer slaves under the law, but a people living in freedom under grace" (*Praeceptum* VIII). The path of reunion carries us along several stages that guide us from the Law to the free imitation of Christ to His eventual intervention in the form of Grace: "And walk in love, as Christ loved us and gave himself up for us, a fragrant offering and sacrifice to God" (Ephesians 5:2). To accompany——to become——the pilgrims, the

---

[10]The theory of language at play directly derives from the idea of truth as *aletheia*—unveiling—present in the New Testament. Signs may veil truth due to insufficiency or intentions. Sometimes, we just cannot express something properly; our words fail us, or we fail them. Other times, we choose words to indirectly guide others toward meaning: "now there are two reasons why written texts are not understood: Either they are veiled in unknown signs or in ambiguous ones. Now signs are either literal or metaphorical. They are said to be literal when they are used as signs for those things they were originally intended to point to" (*On Christian Teaching* X.10.15). This level of meaning and rule following matches Wittgenstein's ostension: Signs mean by pointing at things in a world that we assume to be real. The deeper level of language in Augustine does no longer pertain to how signs in the world indicate things in the world but is instead concerned with how signs in the world point at the very possibility of the world. God's perfume, present in all of language, makes interpretive path feasible for Augustine.

shining fragrance helping the monastery to become the house where God's people reunite among themselves and reunite with the Lord. His fragrance is an evanescent force that guides humans back to where they belong. The West may be a visual culture for which thinking is seeing—eidos—but the sense of smell has always had a special place in the culture of religious offerings: "Then Aaron's sons shall burn it on the altar upon the burnt offering, which is upon the wood on the fire; it is an offering by fire, a pleasing odor to the Lord" (Leviticus 3:5). For ages, the fragrance of sacred holocaust has been a powerful means of communication with the divine. If humans have communicated with the Highest by ritually burning animal fat, imagine what God might be able to do with His divine perfume.

The Bible—and all of human language for that matter—encloses the perfume of God's language. A form of language of its own, smell has the advantage of cutting through the confusion of dissenting tongues and imperfect human communication. Not even the tumultuous rumor of Babylon can deafen the penetrating fragrance of the divine. There is one last offering, then. Lambs give way to the Lamb that makes Himself wholly present for one final divine sacrifice. The book of Revelation speaks of one last temple after the Temple. Human buildings will fall, but the temple of the heart reigns eternal; as the evangelist reaches the ultimate vision of the perfect city, "I saw no temple in the city, for its temple is the Lord God the Almighty and the Lamb [. . .] But nothing unclean shall enter it, nor any one who practices abomination or falsehood, but only those who are written in the Lamb's book of life" (Revelation 21:22–7). The Book of Life is the book of the definitive Lamb that gives His life to and for us. Ungrateful and self-inclined as we are, Augustine exhorts us to try to imitate Christ's self-holocaust, according to our possibilities. Following the rule, an exercise that can only be completed in common demands that we offer ourselves in one last, imitative sacrifice to build the city of New Jerusalem. Saint Augustine calls it the Kingdom of Love.

3

Kingdom of Love

Interpretation and the Kingdom of Love

Wittgenstein identified a theory of language in Augustine's *Confessions*. He was right. Ostension and signs constitute the daily bread and butter of human communication. Wittgenstein's quarrel with miscommunication and false philosophical problem, however, is not one leveled against Augustine's ideas. In fact, both thinkers question the validity of self and signs. They, too, expose those who follow empty rules of life: "These precepts should be read to you once a week, so that you will see yourselves in this little book as in a mirror and not neglect anything through forgetfulness. When you find yourselves doing what has been written here, thank the Lord, the giver of all good gifts" (*Praeceptum* VIII.2).[1] Being free is doing what has been written. What makes Augustine's books on language, exegesis, and teaching the masterpieces have to do with the place that he saves for language. Exegesis must lead to love.

Saint Augustine's potent theory of teaching yields a fruitful model of interaction with the world: the world and its underlying causes, the Book of Nature, are here to be read, to be interpreted. The solution lies in interpretation. If the world is a book, the Book of Nature, and our lives are somehow connected to the Book of Life, our path to the Creator will have to traverse the road from the

---

[1] "Ut autem uos in hoc libello tamquam in speculo possitis inspicere, ne per obliuionem aliquid neglegatis, semel in septimana uobis legatur. Et ubi uos inueneritis ea quae scripta sunt facientes, agite gratias domino bonorum omnium largitori" (*Praeceptum* VIII.2).

signs, to their inner perfume, to, ultimately, the author. Consistently, interpreting does not just mean exegesis or hermeneutics chez Augustine; on the contrary, to interpret means to dive into the code of existence, inhabit it, and learn to find love in the universal language which structures and makes it all possible. This code is legated to us in creation and Scripture. The only viable school of exegesis will be one that, when facing the tantalizing signs of world and text, makes finding the underlying—yet in plain sight discernible—love at the heart of language: "so when dealing with figurative expressions, follow this as a basic rule: that the text being read should be turned over and over, considered diligently for a long while, until your interpretation can be led over into the kingdom of love" (*On Christian Teaching* III.15.23). The purpose of language is to ask questions to learn and teach. The ultimate purpose of language is to guide us to the Kingdom of Love.

Augustine's theory of interpretation exhorts us to treat the world as a most beautiful book that demands to be read. Eventually, all true reading must evince the underlying code—the engram—of all existence, which is the Book of Nature. Developing an understanding of this universal language and logic naturally leads to falling in love with the maker of one such code. Interpreting is reading the world and finding love for the Creator in every verse. Because this creation is itself an expression of unconditional love, readers of the world grammar must also follow Christ's admonition to love God and neighbor. A proper interpretation of the texts of Scripture and nature must lead exactly to the fulfillment of the great commandment: "So whoever, in his own view, thinks he has understood the divine scriptures, or some part of them, and yet does not, by his interpretation, build up the twofold love of god and neighbor, then that person has not yet understood the text," contends Augustine (36.40). There is no other reason for speaking, reading, or writing. Not even for living. Love is the meaning and the reason.

In order to unveil the love at the heart of all language, we must fall afresh in love with "the means that carry us along" (26.27). Human language, even in its most beautiful expression, is a vehicle. But that does not mean that we should deprecate it because of its finitude, imprecision, and unreliability. We should learn to love it for what it is so that we can be grateful for the gift and praise the gifter. All too often, however, we forget about the universal language present in all things and start believing that we are the source of our knowledge. In some cases, we attribute this to other mortals to the point of undeserved glorification. Very often, the illusion of lofty wisdom—for our species does not really know much about anything—makes us erect ourselves as our own golden calves of adoration and idolatry.

A lover of wisdom above most, Augustine always maintained a serene, healthy skepticism regarding the reach of human endeavors. Even as a figure dedicated to seeking and sharing knowledge, he was able to write very harsh pages regarding the prideful practice of many masters and teachers. He warns us against those who follow empty rules and those who claim to be the wisest:

> Do teachers ever claim that it is their own thoughts that are grasped and retained, rather than the branches of learning themselves which they purport to transmit by their speaking? What foolish curiosity could ever prompt a man to send his child to school in order to have him learn what the teacher thinks? But when teachers have made use of words to explain all those branches of learning which they profess to be teaching, including even those dealing with virtue and wisdom, then those who are known as pupils reflect within themselves whether what has been said is true, contemplating, that is, that inner truth according to their capacity. It is then, therefore, that they learn. And when they discover within themselves that what has been said is true, they praise their teachers, unaware that they are not so much praising the teachers as they are praising those who have been taught. (*The Teacher* 59)

This paragraph entails a complete theory of language, teaching, and learning. First, nobody owns the truth. The truth owns us. Second, the best teachers are those who acknowledge their role as inspirators and guides in a process that is ultimately an inner dialogue between the soul and God. Third, finding truths is unveiling them. We merely discover it. The process is individual because it is the soul that is involved in the holy dialogue, but we need others to guide us, both for learning and living, for it is their caring questioning that elevates us to a stage of proper knowledge and appreciation.

To follow a rule we first need to be able to read the rule. The teacher is Augustine the homodiegetic narrator, who teaches us what language is in the form of a dialogue between Augustine

and Adeodatus, who was his son and the youngest member of the
Cassiciacum koinon established by Augustine. The homodiegetic
father and his son discuss in a Socratic manner about the role
of questions on our journey toward wisdom: "Augustine. 'What
would you say we are trying to do whenever we speak?' Adeodatus.
'As it strikes me right now, we want either to teach or to learn.'
Aug. 'I see, and I agree with one of these, but how does this hold
for learning?' Ad. 'How in the world do you suppose we learn, if
not by asking questions?'" (*The Teacher* 7). Asking questions is the
only path toward learning and teaching, operations which in turn
epitomize the purpose of language. If speaking is learning, who
will ask the best questions? The person who loves us the most. A
loving mother, a true friend, a caring teacher. Their good questions
are an irreplaceable scaffold built out of the echo of the only true
Teacher's words. Somewhat correcting the unidimensional picture
of Augustine's theory transmitted by Wittgenstein, the saint warns
us against excessive attachment to earthly words and masters:

> For the present, I have cautioned you that we must not ascribe
> more importance to words than is their due. Accordingly, we
> should no longer merely believe, but also begin to understand the
> truth of those words based on divine authority, that we should
> not call any man on earth a teacher, seeing that "there is One in
> heaven who is the Teacher of all" (Matt. 23:9). (*The Teacher* 60)

Strictly speaking, there is only one teacher. The rest of us who live
in language are echoes and vessels. Still, we are given the choice to
become luminous vessels sailing toward his truth, or calamitous
vehicles striding toward inexorable wreckage. Ultimately, teachers
do not hand us the truth on a silver plate. The good ones will help
us ask the right questions inside. The same questions that Augustine
was taught how to ask toward the end of the chronological portion
of the *Confessions*, in whose books VIII and IX he met the inspiring,
imitable figures that led to his conversion. None of those masters
saw themselves as masters, but as ushers in the House of God.

Teachers help us open doors and encourage us to cross them.
Likewise, God could have easily given us perfection. As much as
there is a difference separating pagan from biblical teachers, there
is one separating pagan deities from the monotheistic God. The
former create other gods for their own gratification and delight;

that is why we have theogonies, pantheons, and sagas. The latter could have created more powerful and perfect divine companions for Himself. A perfect creation of perfect beings could appear to be a greater act of love than the—perfect—creation of imperfect, fallible, and mortal humans. Yet, His wisdom is greater. Our limited vision might render this finitude as a missed opportunity or an act of disdain. On the contrary, by not giving us perfection upfront, the perfect Teacher is conferring us the greatest of privileges: The journey of learning toward the Kingdom of God. For we only teach, truly teach, those who we love the most; thus, mortality is turning all of creation into a life-long school of endless charity.

The Problem with the *Rule*

Picture a perfect language, teacher, and related form of life. The rule that governs it, the rule that makes it conceivable and possible, needs to be followable. It needs to be followed, too. Interpretation renders this scheme feasible. A monastic rule is a rule that houses its own theory of interpretation and following. Inside Augustine's house, however, lies a potential absurdity, for why would anyone follow a rule—or even write a rule of life—if there is a possibility that everything has already been determined and there might not be anyone—no necessary unification of experience—commanding this rule—follower's semblance of free will?

Saint Augustine's theory of Grace is often seen as a paramount precursor of many Western theories of predestination, which in technical terms is a species of determinism.[2] An intentionally

---

[2]Something is happening in the world today. A sign of the social bodies' ever-growing complexity, more and more members of all faiths abide by metaphysical axioms originating in theoretically opposed cosmovisions. Simultaneously. Let us reflect for a second on the implication of such a fascinating phenomenon. What does it mean for Christians, Jews, or Muslims to believe in karma, luck, or any other notion of freedom and fortune stemming from a different worldview? Even more interestingly, this syncretism is not often discussed. All the more frequently, this is not even realized as a development worth discussing. The impact of twenty-first-century information society on religious dogma is yet to be written, but there is something to be said today about how two incompatible concepts of freedom can coexist in one individual.

directed and oriented form of mechanically determined ontology authored by a higher power. This bewildering gesture in the thought of Augustine warrants the query, why would he ruin or enervate his otherwise solid theory of Grace with a passion for free will?

Even more radically, why would Augustine, or anyone for that matter, compose a *Rule* of life, a manual of existence, if all of life's acts were already determined? In a strictly deterministic system, should we not just go with the flow and follow the script that is handed to us? A perfect script, nonetheless. Why not just be contemplative—maybe even passive—readers instead of writers? The *Rule*'s rendition of the imitative Christian tradition cuts the Gordian knot by proving that humans must simultaneously read the script of the vita Christi and write—transcribe—as close a copy as possible on our vital story.

The tussle between reading life and writing life constitutes one of the greatest theoretical challenges found in Augustine's mature works. In fact, several of his late works contradict not only his previous interpretation of free will but also clash against the very letter of Revelation. Augustine's commentary on Revelation 20:12–15 found in the *City of God* 20.14 forces us to either contravene the words of the New Testament regarding the significance of deeds, redefine the terms involved, or find a way for the names in the Book of Life to be written according to our own deeds. Although not completely clear, there seems to be a way to save free will without theoretically abolishing God's omniscience and omnipotence. The paradox, luckily, is not irremediably unsolvable. We might have been looking in the wrong texts; by focusing on the theoretical treatises in dialogue with *On Free Will*, *On Grace and Free Will*, the *City of God*, or even the early collection addressing *Eighty-three Different Questions*, an opuscule composed to quench the desire for knowledge of the saint's monastic fellows before he delved into formally instituted monasticism, we may have missed the fact that Augustine had already provided us with a solution to the dilemma.

A Rule Is Not a Book

Nowadays known as *Regula Sancti Augustini*, the *Rule* is composed of at least nine overlapping handbooks and letters. The taxon encompasses a relation of works which includes the

Ordo monasterii, Praeceptum, Praeceptum longius, and the latter *Regula recepta*—; five feminine rules entitled *Obiurgatio, Regularis informatio, Epistula longior, Ordo monasterii feminis datus*; and, finally, the *Epistula longissima* (George Lawless, *Augustine of Hippo and His Monastic Rule* 65–72). These magnificent works have been studied mostly from within monastic scholasticism, but their value is universal. Luckily, among these monastic interpreters, we find prominent names such as Adolar Zumkeller (1949 *Das Mönchtum des heiligen Augustinus*), Luc Verheijen (1967 *La règle de Saint Augustin,* 1979 *Saint Augustine's Monasticism in the Light of Acts 4:32–5,* and 1980 *Nouvelle approche de la règle de Saint Augustin*), Tarsicius J. Van Bavel (1986 *The Rule of Saint Augustine*), and George Lawless (1987 *Augustine of Hippo and His Monastic Rule*). Since these and other commendable contributions have carefully and intelligently unveiled the meaning and history of most of the *Rule's* content, we are now presented with an interpretive opportunity that cannot be missed: The invitation to elucidate the way in which the *Rule* takes the chronological first person of the *Confessions* and turns it into a handbook on how to approach eternity through love.

Toward the end of his life, probably around AD 426 or 427, Augustine composed one of his last major works, entitled *Retractationes.* Translated as *Retreatises, Retreatments,* or *Retractations,* this retrospective collection of commentaries musters a comprehensive, acute judgment of Augustine's own works to date. The project was never culminated, as he notes in an abrupt final paragraph:

> When I reviewed these writings of mine, I found that I had composed ninety-three works in two hundred thirty-two books. I did not know up to that time whether I was going to write others and, on the insistence of my brethren, I published this review of them in two books before beginning to reexamine my letters and my sermons to the people, the former dictated, the latter spoken. (*Retractations* 93.270–1)

There is some recanting, but the main gesture is one of readdressing: convinced that humans can become a bit less unwise over time, Augustine goes back to the things he could have said better, had he been wiser. In doing so, he could just have embraced the bitterness of a repudiated past, but his return to self is a rare case of a fair, insightful perspective. Instead of shunning the actions of selves past, he gives an account of the moment and place that saw the original thought come to life, understands the source of his confusion, and invites the reader to rationally join him in the evolution of his doctrines.

As Augustine revises the mind of the man he used to be, he elides one major work and that is the *Rule*. He does mention treatises and books, plus he overtly acknowledges his inability to cover his more than 276 letters and 1,000 sermons to date, but nothing is said about any of the letters, manuscripts, and documents that form the *Regula Sancti Augustini*. Considering that different versions of the rule had been circulating since around the turn of the century and some of the pertinent letters were dated in the early 420s, this comes as a tantalizing absence.

What is the cause of this omission? For the most part, his retrospective reappraisal only pays attention to the works he intended to legate in writing, which encompasses his dictations and his own writings; however, he recognizes that some of the things he said were put into writing, regardless of his intentions.[3] Although he does not adopt as radical a position as Plato's theory of writing in the contentious *Seventh Letter*, Augustine does not include most sermons and letters in the anthology of retracted materials. This could disallow two of the epistles—*Epistula longior* and *Epistula longissimi*—where several of the *Rule*'s versions originated, but not all, given that at least a few of the preceptive works he composed were explicitly intended to be read by the target monastic community. Even the general version of the rule—the *Praeceptum*—includes a proposition reminding readers of their duty to reread the text every week: "These precepts should be read to you once a week, so that

---

[3]The distinction between oral—that which is simply said—dictated—that which is said to be transcribed— and written is fully present in the Retractation's "Prologue": "I have written a great deal, or even because many things which I did not dictate, but which I said, were put into writing for when necessary things are said, God forbid that this be considered wordiness, no matter how prolix or loquacious it may be" (*Retractations*, "Prologue" 4). On another level, three of the works glossed in the *Retractations* are connected by their relation to the monasteries of Carthage and Hadrumetum in modern Tunisia. Chapters "47. *On the Work of Monks*," "92. *On Grace and Free Will*," and "93. *On Admonition and Grace*" address the controversies regarding manual labor and mendicant contemplation, as well as its higher order framework, the problem of Grace and free will.

you will see yourselves in this little book as in a mirror and not neglect anything through forgetfulness" (*Praeceptum* VIII.2). As much as the self is auto-opaque but translucent to others, the rule has to be read to us. The *Rule*'s language game is one where there is no possible private language. As a book, it can only work for a community of readers.

Truthfully, the rules are by definition a living—a lived—unfinished product. Incompleteness, however, did not prevent him from including Retractations on truncated works such as *One Unfinished Book on the Literal Meaning of Genesis*. Irrespective of considering it an "inperfectus" draft, Augustine recognizes that he "decided to keep it so that it might serve as evidence, useful in my opinion, of my first attempts to explain and search into the divine Scriptures" (*Retractations* 17.76–7). Apart from including imperfect, unfinished works, he also lists one piece as "incoata," inchoated, *An Unfinished Explanation of the Epistle to the Romans* (Chapter 24), prefaced by saying: "discouraged by the magnitude and labor of this task, I stopped adding other volumes to explain the entire Epistle, and I lapsed into easier things. And thus it happened that I left a single book, the first one I composed. I determined that its title should be: *An Unfinished Explanation of the Epistle to the Romans*" (*Retractations* 24.105). Even the extraordinary *Soliloquies*, the true history of the soul's combat, are added to the corpus undeterred by the fact that it "has remained unfinished" (4.16). Despite most of the sources bequeathed adopting the format of scholarly monographs and theological treatises, there are various types of texts including exegeses, acts, proceedings, replies, dialogues, and questions. Due to their intended purpose and form of transmission, most sermons and letters are missing. The proliferation of texts related to the *Rule*, however, renders the absence of the nine preceptive manuscripts a puzzling reality. The *Rule* is a text governed by a temporality that is not that of chronology. If that is the case, it would make sense that the *Retractations*, a chronological review of Augustine's own texts, would not register this piece, for the *Rule* does not exactly inhabit time.[4]

---

[4]Current scholarship on the *Retractations* highlights the chronological nature of the saint's retrospective compilation: "The central theme of the Dialogue is succinctly stated in the *Retractations*, a chronological review of the Saint's works, exclusive of

The aspect of the compositive process and the nature of the sources are not the reason why the rules are not exhibited as part of his self-reflecting legacy. Neither does his authorial intent, or lack thereof, to publish or circulate his manuscripts prevent him from including a treatise we came to know and treasure:

> After the books, *Soliloquies,* and after my recent return from the country to Milan, I wrote a book, *On the Immortality of the Soul.* I had intended this as a reminder to me, so to speak, to complete the *Soliloquies,* which had remained unfinished; but it fell, I know not how, into the hands of men against my will and is listed among my works. First of all, because of the intricacy and brevity of its reasoning, it is so obscure that even my attention flags as I read it and I, myself, can scarcely understand it. (*Retractations* 5.20)

In several occasions, Augustine did not only consider a past manuscript as unconcluded, but also unworthy: "while I was re-examining my writings in the present work, this very book came into my hands, unfinished as it was, which I had not published and which I had decided to destroy" (17.76). Nothing of the sort happened regarding the different rules found in letters and scripts.

Was his saintly modesty what prevented him from even conceiving that, thousands of years later, thousands of fellows would still live their lives according to the humble precepts he formulated for a community of friends who gathered around him?[5] While readers and scholars have rejoiced in the depth of the *Confessions* and the *City of God,* no Augustinian text has transformed more lives than the *Rule.* Yet he did not mention it in his exhaustive intellectual

---

Sermons and *Letters,* composed between 426 and 427. 'During this same period,' he writes, 'I composed a book called *The Teacher* where, after some discussion and inquiry, we find that it is God alone who teaches men knowledge, all of which is also in accord with what is written in the Gospel: 'One is your teacher, Christ'" (*The Teacher* 3, "Introduction").

[5]George Lawless and all rule scholars for that matter stress the saint's "gregarious temperament, Augustine proposed at Milan in the year 386 to live his life in common with then adults. All were friends, and from their number two individuals would be elected annually on a rotation basis, like the Roman magistrates" (*Augustine of Hippo and His Monastic Rule* 3).

homecoming. Truth be told, the *Rule* was never a book. The 387 verses generally known as *Regula Sancti Augustini* in actuality designate a compilation of nine documents including masculine and feminine rules, as well as several letters. A reading of these rules as the natural continuation of the path of self-questioning started in *Confessions* can shed valuable light onto the meaning and motivation at the heart of the *Rule*.

Built upon Verheijen's paradigm-shifting studies which combed through 317 texts, nowadays it is worth adopting Van Bavel's nonagonal interpretive apparatus of Augustine's regulatory writings (*La règle de Saint Augustin* 17–24). According to this hermeneutic school concomitantly embraced by George Lawless, there is not one monolithic rule, but the monastic *propositum* of unconditional love spoused by Saint Augustine is one that emerges across all manuscripts (*Augustine of Hippo and His Monastic Rule* 65–7). Coherently, the heterogeneous and interspersed nature of Augustine's regulatory literature is not sufficient to cause for his omission from the *Retractations*. *On Hellenism, Judaism, Individualism, and Early Christian Theories of the Subject*, a volume that complements the present one, saw me arguing that Augustine did not see the *Rule* as a literary product subject to retraction ("Chapter IV. Monasticism"). I also insinuated that the *Rule* was the only nonliterary member in Augustine's complete corpus. When Augustine decided not to readdress the *Rule* in the *Retractations*, he knew what he was doing. Why? Because a rule might be more than a book.

A rule is not a book. One does not just read a rule. Rules are followed. We follow them. Or we do not. Rules may or may not be used. In any case, reading them is not using them. And using them does not require me to read them; in fact, Augustine does not expect the *Rule* to be read, but weekly hearkened, "These precepts should be read to you once a week" (*Praeceptum* VIII.2). A rule is a text that demands readers to write their own book, which is life.

A rule is a ladder. Like a tool, intended and actual use might or might not match in real life. Using tools and reading about tools—or, much more interestingly, reading tools—are by no means one and the same, so reading a rule and using a rule must be understood in their own terms. A rule is a ladder that contains a map. The frameworks of performativity and declarative speech acts get us closer to what is at stake, but these paradigms ultimately fail to capture the *Rule*'s essential principle: The *Rule* is to be followed by someone else, not me. Unlike an instruction manual—a rulebook that does not change the subject holding it, but the subject's command of a technique or technology—a monastic rule is a book that no reader can follow, for they will become someone else just by following the rule. Technically speaking, nobody can follow Augustine's rules because no subject will be the same after following them. Nobody climbs the ladder, for everyone will have become someone else by the time we take the last step.

A rule is a knife. Not in the sense of Augustine's just war theory or playfully invoking any alluring twists on his zealous defense of all life as worthy. There is no paradox here, for the *Rule* is a weapon with only one intended use, which is suicide. Or more precisely, the mystical death of the self—*mors mystica*—, a mystical suicide heralding the death of the former egotistic self. The *Rule*'s toolbox performs two creatively destructive tasks. It kills that which is false in us and maieutically helps give birth to a new, truer self.

A rule cannot succeed. The most alluring realization accompanying the *Rule* is that it is a tool and a knife necessarily bound to fail. Because its language game is mankind, the rule cannot really kill the old self for as long as we are alive. If we live for our time, it fails. If it succeeds, we are not here to see it. Wittgenstein addresses this problem in the last pages of the *Tractatus*: "Death is not an event in life: we do not live to experience death. If we take eternity to mean not infinite temporal duration but timelessness, then eternal life belongs to those who live in the present. Our life has no end in just the way in which our visual field has no limits" (§6.4311). This means that those problems susceptible to being formulated are necessarily answerable problems; everything that falls beyond the realm of proper language, we call it the mystical.

The beauty of monastic rules is that each attempt brings forth a slightly improved version of the self whose readers aspire to become, but never a perfect one. Just like the pulse between the two egos of the *Soliloquies* and the *Confessions*, each weekly re-reading of the *Rule* kills a greater portion of the former, vain self and animates a growing identity based on the independence from everything that is superfluous—fame, quarrels, luxury, entertainment, self. As simple as it might seem, one of the hardest challenges found in every monastic rule—and constitution for that matter—is the definition of the fundamental, non-superfluous, and so-called natural axioms of human life. Augustine's *Rule* deals with the bare foundation and solves the issue the Stoic way, "For it is better to need less than to have more" (*Praeceptum* III.5). Whereas most constitutions, rules, and declarations of rights tend to immovably define what is necessary and what is not, the saint equips his brothers and sisters with a perennially flexible criterion to demarcate what is necessary and what is not. Instead of having to rewrite the rule every time a new "need" arises, Augustine expects coenobites to be ambitious, yet reasonable in their adaptation to the medium. Despite not being an excessively ascetic rule, Augustine does continue with the intuition at Cassiciacum where the saint realized that he would only fully find God and himself when subtracted from the otiose turb. That is why, while being generous but sober with food and clothing, instead of entertainment, Augustine exhorts us not to be present in the interstice implied in enter-tainment, but to make ourselves present in full "tainment" or attainment.

A rule is never mine. The life under the rule is the closest to the mirror of eternity and its perfect, absolute present. God, however, gives humans freedom because He wants us to try; he also gives us Grace because He knows we will fail. A monastic rule cannot succeed, but it can get us closer and closer to eternity so that when God's Grace has to eventually—and certainly—come to save us, we will have given everything we had. Even more interestingly, this state of being doomed to try and fail and try and fail and try and fail yields a self that is not strictly individual. The certainty of failure serves to expose a fundamental lie often fought by Augustine's first-person writing, that is, the idea that there is something essentially mine in *my*self: "Hence, I would not be, my God, I would not be at all, unless Thou wert in me" and "Thou wert within and I was without" (*Confessions* I.2.2; X.27.38). Reading the *Confessions* and the *Rule* as biographical writing misses the part of humans as usufructuaries who use and possess the self, but in no way own it as ex-cathedra property. For the self to be truly mine is to realize that *my*self is not mine.

A rule is not in time. The Rule is not a book. It is also a work that does not exist in time. This history of life outside chronology departs from the assumed conversion of the *Confessions*; in fact, it is a prerequisite for brothers and sisters to have walked their own journey of conversion, since adhesion to the monastery must be the freest of acts. After the conversion, time changes. Our mortal chronology is exposed as insufficient and a novel, radical commitment to the present moment must commence. The first nine books of the *Confessions* embody Augustine's last biographical text in its linear sense. Having overcome finitude in the realm of theory, he is now able to embark on composing the next kind of life-writing where there is no chronology, which is the artificial—fallen—separation of past, present, and future. Thus, the *Rule* emerges as an attempt to write a biography that transcends human time. A life outside time and chronology. As such, it is a biography of everyone's eternal present.

By tapping into the divine text of the world, the Book of Nature, Saint Augustine is able to formulate a biography of times to come. He closes the work by recognizing the power of looking forward and backward so that we can learn from our mistakes: "let him be sorry for the past, safeguard the future, and continue to pray," Augustine asserts (*Praeceptum* VIII.1). The original Latin phrasing comprises a telling tense change that embodies Augustine's entire theory of time: "doleat de praeterito, caueat de futuro, orans." The present active participle form is a marvelous tense that most romance languages eventually lost in favor of its adjectival and nominal application. There is a sense of living—verb—actor—noun—that even in English has residually yielded words such as orans, orant, and orator. In any case, should one of the sisters or brothers make a mistake, a serene but cautious look at the past and future must necessarily give way to an attitude of prayer and forgiveness that embodies the plenitude of the present besought by Saint Augustine. Past and future will soon be seen as a speck when compared to the fullness—the absolute presence—of God's eternity being made present here and now.

Past and future are still recognized as part of our human chronology. We might indeed never be able to get rid of them, but Augustine's honesty here does not prevent him from only attributing past and future their due, moderate importance; consistently, past and future are only to be considered when we fail. They too are ladders, tools, and rules to help transport us back to the ascending path. Once we fail—which we will—let us serenely but briefly learn from the past and look at the future so that we can focus on the ultimate goal of monastic life, which is the construction of a never-ending present. The cycles described by Augustine and other, more legalistic rules, are precisely designed to imitate the feel of eternity.

A cycle—the daily labor, prayers, and the ebb and flow of meals and fasts—is the best approach we have to the static, calm nature of the flowless eternal.

Instead of blindly speculating, it is easier to live a good life if we live it while reading the infallible script of what life should be which, for the Eastern tradition and Augustine's pioneering work in Western monasticism, is no other than Christ's own life. An autobiography of the future, but not a prophecy, for the *Rule* does not tell us what will happen, but instead what shall happen. The monastic tradition might have found the perfect rule to follow in the vita Christi. Now we just need to follow it; which is easier said than done.

Do as Written

If life is written, why do we insist on calling it free will? Seneca, Calvin, Spinoza. Their solutions to the dilemma are neat and ontologically parsimonious. Erasing or profoundly redefining free will—the power to write a new script—is a coherent and consistent way to ensure God's unnegotiable attribute of omniscience and omnipotence. Among infinite attributes that escape the human mind, God's absolute power must be an absolute power to do—omnipotence—and to know—omniscience. If handed a script—the perfect script in a metaphysically, almost Leibnizian sense of optimism—authored by an infallible hand, how could a mere human being claim to—or even want to—alter the course of time? How could our fallible handwriting enrich or redact the already immaculate text of creation? All verses, all of life's actions coming from such a negligible creature would blush when collated with God's absolute command of beauty. At best, our contributions to the text of nature might become blots in an otherwise immaculate work of art. Well aware of the weight of the saeculum—life that fails to see eternity in chronology–, the *Rule* contemplates the possibility of readers not living the life therein characterized. Hence, a paradoxical statement closes the work as Augustine instructs his brothers and sisters: "When you find yourselves doing what has been written here, thank the Lord, the giver of all good gifts" (*Praeceptum* VIII.2). The secret of Christian imitation, the broader stream containing all monastic

rules, is that eternity—universal harmony and concord in love—
is already taking place.

The *Rule* apprises its readers of the fact that the life of Christ
which Christians strive to imitate is the biography everyone should
want their autobiographies to become. If successful, the two
should eventually be one. As expected, the fallen nature of human
finitude prevents this identification from ever fully happening, but
the *Rule* is there to remind everyone that trying is all we have.
Living a good life is, then, writing life according to the already
written life of Christ. This is why Augustine tells us to thank the
Lord whenever we find ourselves living according to the script
which has been written for us. Each life has been written, yet it is
still everyone's duty to write it every day. Even though *imitation*
is the term most often used to describe the endeavor to live a life
like Christ's, *transcription* is a more powerful concept. As scholars
and scribes do in a library; as promoter DNA does in the realm
of genetics; monks, maybe all of us, are called to take the text of
Christ's life and inscribe it onto their skins. Scripturally speaking,
the name of God is inscribed on each of our foreheads for our
salvation.

Reading the *Rule* finally becomes following the *Rule*; a path to
imitate a life with which we are already very familiar. Thus, the
differences across the myriad of monastic orders and rules are but
the differences in the path and methodology to make the imitation
of Christ succeed. The goal is one, but not all approaches triumph
over the limitations of human mutability. Convinced that we are
stronger together and nobody can be a complete Christian without
someone else to serve and love—a lesson monks learned from Saint
Basil—the Augustinian method strives to imitate Christ by first
reproducing the community of believers that most closely followed
the steps of Christ's life. The koinonia of Jerusalem characterized
in Acts of the Apostles 4:32–5 is thus seen as the most promising
ladder to take us to the New Jerusalem of Revelation 21:1–8.[6]

---

[6]Rousseau's *Discourse on the Origin and Foundations of Inequality Among Mankind*
proposes a taxonomy of selfishness—also translated as vanity—and self-love: "We
must not confuse selfishness with self-love; they are two very distinct passions both in
their nature and in their effects. Self-love is a natural sentiment, which inclines every
animal to look to his own preservation, and which, guided in man by reason and
qualified by pity, is productive of humanity and virtue. Selfishness is but a relative

Prescribed Freedom

The possibility of life being written entails serious, far-reaching consequences. Regarding, for example, the nature of the author, an evil genius might very well be controlling each one of our thoughts. If life is a simulation and we happen to be nothing more than brains in a vat, as Hillary Putnam (1926–2016) spurs us to consider, would words such as "free," "good" and "bad," "right" and "wrong" mean anything at all? A thoroughly deterministic world such as that of a pre-recorded simulation of impressions could very well include the illusion of morality, freedom, and agency; should the—probably evil—playwright controlling our thoughts and acts have so decided.

René Descartes (1596–1650) might have written the *Discourse on the Method of Rightly Conducting One's Reason and of Seeking Truth in the Sciences* in a completely different environment, but in 1637 the philosopher was already well aware of the moral and political implications of mechanical philosophy. Descartes's solution, or lack thereof, to the problem of positing a moral system in an incomplete state of human knowledge is the well-known provisional model, "moral par provision" (*Discours* III.39). This gesture is often glossed in regard to Descartes's ultimate acceptance of existing norms and customs, but it is easy to overlook the fact that he is perfectly aware of this position's power against the possibility of all things being mechanically determined. In a Stoic turn that Cartesian

---

and factitious sentiment, engendered in society, which inclines every individual to set a greater value upon himself than upon any other man, which inspires men with all the mischief they do to each other, and is the true source of what we call honor. This position well understood, I say that selfishness does not exist in our primitive state, in the true state of nature; for every man in particular considering himself as the only spectator who observes him, as the only being in the universe which takes any interest in him, as the only judge of his own merit, it is impossible that a sentiment arising from comparisons, which he is not in a condition to make, should spring up in his mind. For the same reason, such a man must be a stranger to hatred and spite, passions which only the opinion of our having received some affront can excite; and as it is contempt or an intention to injure, and not the injury itself that constitutes an affront, men who don't know how to set a value upon themselves, or compare themselves one with another, may do each other a great deal of mischief, as often as they can expect any advantage by doing" (146). Published in the 1980s, a seminal article by Peter Fuss, entitled "Rousseau's Engagement with Amour-Propre," is still a most appropriate source in the study of vanity and self-love chez Rousseau.

continuator Baruch Spinoza (1632–77) would advance to its ultimate consequences, Descartes recognizes that he is betting on the care of the self as the only certain battleground against necessity; not able to really know who or what controls our actions, he promises to vanquish himself and his desires instead of futilely trying to change the course and fate of the world: "Ma troisième maxime était de tâcher toujours plutôt à me vaincre que la fortune, et à changer mes désirs que l'ordre du mon" (*Discours* III.44).

Over time, more coherent Cartesians than Descartes himself, including Spinoza, but also Baron d'Holbach (1723–89) and Julien Offray de La Mettrie (1709–51), would erect complete political and ethical theories based on the possibility of a strictly deterministic or mechanistic reality. The question, thus, still stands: Do "freedom," "right," and "wrong" mean anything at all if none of our illusory choices were ever the product of our free will?

Another contemporary of Descartes, Nicolas Malebranche (1638–1715), offered a thought-provoking, today understudied answer to this dilemma. A synthesis of Augustinian theology crafted to tackle the challenges of modern mechanical philosophy, Malebranche's theory of occasionalism posits that human decisions and actions are the conduit for God's agency, only true form of causation, to intervene. Occasionalism is one of the most aesthetically pleasing metaphysical theories ever conceived, but it is far from unbreakable. Even though it offered a historically valuable response to blind mechanicism, occasionalism, or whatever other models of human-God interface we may posit, this theory still does not answer the fundamental question of the value of morality in a potentially deterministic universe.

Saint Augustine, who had devoted his adulthood to living a good life, ended up facing a similar dilemma that impelled him to choose between God's absolute mercy and mankind's power of choice. If God is omnipotent, does He then choose not to determine some events—and only some—belonging to His plan? If so, does He only leave as open-ended those occurrences corresponding to human actions? Or, even more restrictively, only those related to human occasions for moral causation?

A courageous treatise by Linda Trinkaus Zagzebski (born in 1946), *The Dilemma of Freedom and Foreknowledge*, published in 1991 makes the case that the tension between divine omnipotence and human free will is, above everything else, a matter of time.

In a commendable gesture of intellectual nobility, Trinkaus does not ultimately commit to any of the models she analyzes. She does present some viable amends to the objections against the models spearheaded by Augustine, Boethius, Aquinas, and Ockham, while opening a few promising doors, but she eventually concedes that there are still major theoretical obstacles to surmount: "the difficulty in seeing *how* God can know the contingent future is probably the most difficult problem for the foreknowledge issue" (*The Dilemma of Freedom and Foreknowledge* 178). Regardless, she makes great progress when she claims that "Foreknowledge is most fundamentally a problem about the structure of time" (178). In an inspired leap, Trinkaus goes back to a problem already present in the last three books of Augustine's *Confessions*; that is, the contrast between the passing, mutable time of humans, and the eternal time of God. By fusing theological tropes with the language of contemporary quantum mechanics, she asserts, "Everything that has been, is now, or will be from the viewpoint of three dimensions is already present to be observed in the fourth dimension [. . .] If time as we know is perspectival, indeed, dependent on a *limited* perspective, we could not very well insist that God should know things from *that* perspective" (178). Despite obviously lacking the quantic approach, centuries ago Augustine had arrived at a similar realization in a most admirable proclamation:

Thou art the highest Being and dost not change, nor is there any completion of today in Thee, yet in Thee it does complete itself, for all these things are in Thee, too. Indeed, they would not have their courses to run unless Thou didst contain them. And, since Thy years do not fail, Thy years are but an ever-present today. How many of our own days, and of our ancestors', have passed through that today of Thine, receiving from it their measures and whatever being they had, while other days are still to pass through and receive their own measures and whatever being will be theirs. "But Thou art always the self-same," and all the things of tomorrow and of the future Thou shalt make today, and all the things of yesterday and of the past Thou hast made today. (*Confessions* I.6.9)

We change, pass, live, and die. God remains. Our mortal, finite, insufficient scope prevents us from grasping all dimensions, all aspects of the absolute. Spinoza would call this immersion in the absolute substance a view sub *specie aeternitatis*. Whereas Spinoza turns God—*Deus sive Natura*—into the unstoppable, absolute force of mechanistic necessity that takes us back to the indifference of the Stoic and Epicurean divinities, Augustine sides with his veterotestamentary heritage as he sees God's free acts of providential Grace as the key to both metaphysics and soteriology. Everything that happens is ultimately an unmerited gift from God. A God, however, that follows the Jewish tradition of the Garden does not just want his rational creatures to blindly obey Him: He wants us to choose to obey Him.[7]

---

[7]According to world-renowned Old Testament scholar, Yehezkel Kaufmann (1889–1963), this is the qualitative difference and greatest innovation of Jewish monotheism. Contrary to the esotericism of ancient secret cults, the monotheistic God encourages knowledge. It is that encouragement which God chooses not to bridle that leads Adam and Eve to taste the form of knowledge of evil that unchains human history as fallen mortals. Kaufmann's exegesis of Genesis is worth its weight in gold: "Only one restriction was placed upon him: he must not, on pain of death, eat of the fruit of the 'tree of knowledge of good and evil.' What is the meaning of this? The intention cannot be to represent God's favorite as bereft of knowledge. To the Bible wisdom is a gift of God; its pursuit is nowhere considered sinful. The Genesis legend itself portrays Adam as having knowledge. From his creation he knew how to work the soil, he could speak, and was able to give names to the animals. Moreover, God's threat and Adam's fear of it presuppose the capacity of distinguishing right from wrong. Eve desired the fruit, not merely for its taste, but because it could make her wise. Such a desire in itself bespeaks an intelligent recognition of knowledge as a good to be sought after. From the beginning, then, man had knowledge of the good and desired it. He knows the difference between life and death, and that death is something to be avoided; but, evil is still veiled from him, because he has never tasted it. His knowledge if; less than that of the celestial beings, for they have divine knowledge of both realms. The tree is conceived, then, not as the source of knowledge in general, but of the knowledge of, and desire for, evil, without which man's comprehension is incomplete. The serpent plays the role of the seducer who reveals evil to man and rouses in him the desire for it. The legend, whose object it is to tell the origin of sin, could not place Adam entirely and essentially beyond the knowledge of evil, because the Bible conceives of sin as a consequence of human freedom, and this has meaning only if good and evil are both within the range of man's experience from the beginning. With great art it symbolizes evil as the tree of knowledge; the tree harbors all evil, for to approach it means to sin, to violate a divine prohibition. Rebellion lay within man's power from the very beginning, and he was unable to stand the test. Defying God, he laid bare the realm of evil, which God had concealed from him without, however, blocking his way to it" (*The Religion of Israel, from Its Beginnings to the Babylonian Exile* 293).

The expectation to freely choose what is right—that is, to freely align with and submit to God's Will—establishes a direct connection between the early choice in front of the Tree of Knowledge of Good and Evil of Genesis 2–3 and the final answerability of Revelation 20, where it is unequivocally proclaimed that we will all be judged according to our deeds. The profound tension between Augustine's confidence in unmerited Grace and his need to recognize the role of deeds assigned by the Scripture leads him to a series of late commentaries in which the tongue of deeds and the tongue of Grace take turns as leaders of a seemingly unsolvable conundrum.[8] The *Rule*, an approximation to the wholly present time of God while still here on earth, is Augustine's solution to that problem. Since our mortal chronology would not run its course had it not been set in motion by God, Augustine incites us to live life knowing that our decaying affairs "would not have their courses to run unless Thou didst contain them" (*Confessions* I.6.9). Without pridefully denying the limitations of our temporality, Augustine encourages readers to found a caritatis societas; a "sanctam societatem" (*Praeceptum* I.7), or a society of love to bridge without breaking the gap between temporality and eternity, freedom, and determinism.

The Augustinian intuition found in his excursus on the nature of time effectively advances the present inquiry. Instead of only

---

[8] The dilemma is only made harder by the fact that Augustine himself expressed a different interpretation in his collection of interrogations, *Eighty-three Different Questions*, composed between 388 and 396, according to the *Retractations*. Question 24, "Do sin and right conduct in result from a free choice of the will?" evinces a view based on merit and proportionality: "everything which is, insofar as it is, is good. For that is supremely good in whose participation other things are good. And everything which is subject to change is good insofar as it exists, though not in and by itself, but by participation in the unchangeable good. In its turn, that good whose participation renders good whatever other things exist is good not by anything other than itself; and this good we also call Divine Providence. Therefore nothing happens in the world by chance. This having been established, it seems to follow that whatever is done in the world is done partly by divine agency and partly by our will. For God is by far incomparably better and more just than any man, no matter how good and just. And the just ruler and governor of all things allows no punishment to be inflicted undeservedly on anyone, nor any reward to be given undeservedly to anyone. That which merits punishment is sin, and that which merits reward is right conduct. And neither sin nor right conduct can be justly charged to anyone who has done nothing of his own will. Accordingly sin and right conduct result from a free choice of the will" (*Eighty-three Different Questions* 50–1).

asking why God would choose to equip His creatures with moral proclivities given the possibility that we might not be free at all, we can now wonder why God might have chosen to only show us a partial aspect of time. A relative perspective that makes us conventionally see past, present, and future as separate stages, as well as perceive cause and effect as the products of human choice. Saint Augustine is convinced that, as the teacher that knows how to guide the student according to the pupil's growing abilities, God decided to allow us to see exactly as much time as our minds would be able to process for our own good. The good teacher is the one who asks, "questions in a way suited to his capacity to learn from his inner light" (*The Teacher* 54). From here, Saint Augustine elaborates a systematic theory of education proportionality and careful scaffolding in *The Teacher* and displays its application in his *Commentary on the Lord's Sermon on the Mount*, where employs the concept to expound on his interpretation of the Jewish and Christian supersession by means of the Sermon on the Mount:

> If inquiry is made as to what the mountain signifies, it is rightly understood to signify the higher precepts of justice, for the precepts that had been given to the Jews were lower. Yet, through His holy prophets and servants and in accordance with a most orderly arrangement of circumstances, the same God gave the lower precepts to a people whom it behooved to be bound by fear; through His Son, He gave the higher precepts to a people whom it befitted to be set free by charity. When lesser things are given to a weaker people and greater things are given to a stronger, they are given by Him who alone knows how to proffer to the human race a medicine adapted to its circumstances. Nor is it any wonder that the same God who has made heaven and earth gives higher precepts for the sake of the kingdom of heaven and lower precepts for the sake of the earthly kingdom (I.2).

This pedagogical progression was fully announced in the Pauline Epistles in the form of a two-stage model of partial, then full knowledge: "For now we see in a mirror dimly, but then face to face. Now I know in part; then I shall understand fully, even as I have been fully understood" (1 Corinthians 13:12). While God did and does observe everything from the nonrelative vision of His absolute eternity, we must strive to transcend the useful but limited boundaries of human temporality as we chase a closer communion with the eternal time of God. We are made finite so we wonder about what is infinite. However, our limited perspective makes us feel all too confident in our partiality, thinking that we are undetermined, autonomous, and self-caused. God's absolute vision shows that only in the meeting of Grace and free will are we saved. In between the two planes, a path, that of Augustine's *Rule*, aimed at overcoming chronology and creating, right here and right now, a present that dreams of being as present as God's perfect, total presence.

An Ever-Present Today

Time is the problem. To triumph over the saeculum.[9] Quietist contemplation and deliberate seclusion; perhaps. Absolute dedication to others to the point of subduing the self-destructive inclinations of the egotistic self; hopefully. Abandonment and surrender to the weight of misplaced love of self; most likely. Overcoming the maladies of the saeculum—finitude that forgets its finitude—ultimately involves a feat that is not within human reach. Having learned to overcome, or at least gain awareness of the weight of the saeculum's chronology—the inability to see God's multifaceted time in all its richness—over the human shoulders in the *Confessions*, Saint Augustine sets out to found a society of love aimed at facilitating "obedience to Thy eternal will, but itself in the temporal order" (*Confessions* XI.6.8). In a most fascinating turn of his exegesis on Genesis, he expounds on a memorable theory of creation in which he wonders what and how God's words

---

[9]Adolar Zumkeller's influential book on Augustine's coenobitism, entitled *Das Mönchtum des heiligen Augustinus*, includes a cunning chapter on the relations between worldly and cloistral living "Welt und Kloster (>saeculum–monasterium<)," a chapter in which the contrast between both forms of life is based on the classical distinction between the century, the time of chronology in the temporal affairs; by taking advantage of this pair of concepts it is time–intuitive but conceptually profound—that, in the form of an analysis of their different temporalities, allows us to expose the different species of love and their objects. Although the time of the saeculum represents the extramural living of those who still have ties of hope or love with the temporal world, there is always hope for a current of eternity to come and touch the order of finite temporality.

instructions for creation might have been uttered. A long passage merits our attention:

> But, how didst Thou speak? Was it in the same way that a voice was produced from the heavens; saying: "This is my beloved Son?" That voice was produced and then was completed; it began and it ended. The syllables sounded and then they passed away; the second followed the first, the third followed the second, and so on in order, until the last syllable followed the rest; then, silence followed the last. From this it is clear and evident that the movement of a creature produced it, in obedience to Thy eternal will, but itself in the temporal order. And the external ear reported these words of Thine, which were made for time, to the prudently reasoning mind whose internal ear is attuned to Thy eternal Word. (*Confessions* XI.6.8)[10]

God's time—Eternity—and God's language—Word—. Their ineffable nature renders all human attempts at grasping them a necessary but necessary failed endeavor. However, Augustine opens an unexpectedly promising door. What if we could align ourselves with eternity, but do so from the temporal order in which we are embedded?

In order to circumvent the weight of temporality, however, we need a proper understanding of the differences between mortal chronology—the distinction of past, present, and future—and eternity—the plenitude of an omni-comprehensive present–. "What, then, is time? If no one asks me, I know; but, if I want to explain it to a questioner, I do not know," Augustine ponders in one of his most celebrated passages (*Confessions* XI.14.17). Such are Augustine's memorable words apropos the elusive nature of time

---

[10]Immediately thereafter, Augustine marvels at the verbal equivalent of seeing God's face; which can be found in the notion of listening to God's words. Is God's language in time? Beyond time? Before time? Augustine posits that the absolute Word of the divine cannot be one subject to the passing and decay of words in chronology: "But this mind compared these words which sound in time with Thy Word, eternal in its silence, and it proclaimed: 'It is different; it is far different. These words are far below me; they do not even exist, for they are fleeting and transitory: 'But the Word of My God endureth above me forever.' [. . .] What Word, then, didst Thou use to create that body whereby those words might be produced?'" (*Confessions* XI.6.8).

but, especially, of eternity. The fracture of the Fall prevents humans from grasping and, all too often, from living according to eternity. We pass; God remains. Yet, anyone who dreams of living closer to eternity will need to realize that it is that same eternity that causes our fallible human chronology. That is exactly what Augustine does in one of the *Confessions'* most memorable passages:

> And behold, my babyhood is long since dead, yet I live. But Thou, O Lord, art ever living and in Thee nothing dies (for before the beginnings of the centuries and before everything which can even be said to be "before," Thou art, and Thou art God and the Lord of all things which Thou hast created, and with Thee the causes of all unstable things stand firm, the immutable sources of all mutable things dwell, and the eternal reasons of all irrational and temporal things live). (*Confessions* I.6.9)

Being is being in time.[11] At least for us, it is. Theologians and philosophers have long debated the place of time in God's creation, as well as the place of God in time; or outside of time. This is a crucial component of the debate involving predestination and the possibility of free will.

That which does not pass, we call eternity. According to Augustine's theological chapters in the *Confessions,* that very eternity is the root of this passing temporality. The saint from Thagaste is demurely aware that creatures cannot just leave time behind and

---

[11]It is just natural that the *Confessions* would eventually seduce those existentialist thinkers preoccupied with the texture of life as a lived temporality, including Soren Kierkegaard, Martin Heidegger, Hannah Arendt, Karl Jaspers, and Paul Ricoeur. This being-in-the-world is established as a passing-in-this-human-time: "if nothing passed away, there would be no past time; if nothing were coming, there would be no future time; and if nothing were existing, there would be no present time. Then, how do those two periods of time, the past and the future, exist, when the past is already not existing, and the future does not yet exist? And again, the present would not pass away into the past, if it were always present; indeed, it would not be time but eternity" (*Confessions* XI.14.17). What if we could devise a form of life that ceased the mere passing of time and allowed us to fully be in the present? The cycles of monastic life and the suspension of the self in divine and fraternal love nurture a new understanding of the present. A temporality that modestly transcends temporality by fully focusing on the present hour, the presence of God here and now, instead of losing ourselves in the trifle vicissitudes of past and future projections.

freely venture into the realm of eternity. A miraculous suspension of temporal chronology or a rapturous glance at the eternal might allow mystics to ephemerally see our mortal temporality subverted. Aside from such mystical ecstasies, the final prophecy of Revelation resolves that we are to live in time—in this mortal time of ours—until the Seventh Seal is opened (Revelation 8:1–6). As much as the unfolding of Revelation, we must be born in this time so that we can learn from the passing of things. The Tree of Knowledge of Good and Evil is also the trunk that can transport us back to a time where time was not time. In the meantime, Saint Augustine's *Rule* acts as a ladder designed to make us a bit less time-sensitive and a lot more eternity-sensitive.

4

The Skin of Heaven

Genealogy of Divine Writing

A rule is a gathering of readable principles to be enacted. Sub *specie aeternitatis*, everything is a rule in the Book of Nature or Creation, since everything can be read. If God has written everything in the form of a universal grammar and syntax, all of nature is a book that can be read and lived. If we possess the code, that is. Augustine's plan of fraternal love on our way toward the divine is an attempt to capture the form of life which is the most conforming to our best attempt at trying to decipher God's Will through reading the Book of Creation. However, our limited lens prevents us from being able to completely decipher the code of existence. We fail to identify true freedom and subject ourselves to our own, consuetudinary golden calves: "The Lord grant you the grace to observe these precepts with love as lovers of spiritual beauty, exuding the fragrance of Christ in the goodness of your lives; you are no longer slaves under the law, but a people living in freedom under grace" (*Praeceptum* VIII.1).[1] How can we discern freedom from slavery? To be fair, thinkers have always been aware of the discrepancy between the gnoseological state in which we are and that in which we would like to be. What behooves us now is analyzing the forms in which this decalage was addressed by the forerunners of the oecumene leading to Saint Augustine's fourth

---

[1]"Donet dominus, ut obseruetis haec omnia cum dilectione, tamquam spiritalis pulchritudinis amatores et bono Christi odore de bona conuersatione flagrantes, non sicut serui sub lege, sed sicut liberi sub gratia constitute" (*Praeceptum* VIII.1).

and fifth-century works. His theory of the divine-human interface within the monastic community would not have been possible without the pagan, Jewish, and Christian substratum underpinning his evolving worldview. Coherently, it is time for us to scrutinize how those before Augustine had conceptualized the notion of life being somehow a matter of language.

Even though most of the Augustinian sources are biblical and classical in origin, in order to unearth the concept of existential writing of the biblical sources, we ought to have a critical look at the following paradigms: (a) the mythical cycle of *Enuma Elis*, which incarnates the first stable paradigm of divine writing incorporated into a cosmological model; (b) the incommensurability of pagan and scriptural writing regarding the determination of human and divine lives; (c) two Old Testament episodes of divine inscription in the books of Exodus, Deuteronomy, and Daniel; (d) the qualitative transformation undergone in Proverbs 3:1–5; (e) the mystery of Incarnation as the transformation from rule-to-be-obeyed into a rule-to-be-imitated.

The Tablets of Destiny: Paganism and Predestination

The theogony of *Enuma Elis* is one of humanity's oldest myths. In usual cosmogonical fashion, tablets dating from three distinct periods between 1300 and 700 BC recount the world's primordial passage from chaos to order.[2] Mesopotamians, Sumerians, Akkadians, Babylonians, Canaanites, or Assyrians are just a few of the Ancient Near Eastern peoples linked to the Olympic league of *Enuma Elis*, a corpus of four-millennia-old traditions which predates and incarnates a trait central to most cosmogonies to come; namely, the conviction that life and our destinies are written. As chaos gives way to order, the fabric of existence becomes textual and the power of the gods is expressed through the act of writing fate itself.

---

[2]The dates surrounding the *Enuma Elis* tablets have been carefully studied by Wilfred G. Lambert, whose monumental *Babylonian Creation Myths* will be followed in all related matters. A chronology of the production and reception of the tablets is provided in the "Introduction: The Text of Enūma Eliš" (*Babylonian Creation Myths* 3–4).

Enuma Elis presents an archetypical plot that cannot but sound familiar. Following a primigenial state of nothingness and disorder, a god chooses to beget the world and beings. At some point, a power struggle leads the original divine kingdom to be seized by a younger, more potent deity. One such reckless god then proceeds to configure the world as our human ancestors first knew it. After the birth of order out of chaos, the new pantheon and the human race—often, a chosen people—start interspersing, acquainting themselves with each other, and delineating the boundaries that demarcate what is human and what is divine. Such is the beginning of history, along with the point of departure for most ancient myths. This pre-human Urgeschichte is necessary for human history to be set in motion. Once the triumphant god has established supreme power by setting the new universal laws in stone, only then can humans continue the lineage by starting to write their own version of those laws in the form of myths, sagas, tablets, codes, histories, and sacred texts. In the end, those capable of claiming the power of writing time will prevail. Variations of this canon can be found at the forefront of most ancient cosmogonies. At their core, there is a preeminence of divine writing as a necessary condition for any human writing to see the light of day. Scriptural exegesis, divination, oracles, omens, prophecies. All are techniques aimed at unveiling, reading, and interpreting the foundational text of the cosmos. The founding code is at the heart of each one of us.

A member of this cosmogonic family, the Mesopotamian order is founded on a verbal act. It is the writing of destinies on the Tablets of Enuma Elis that sets human history in motion. This seemingly inconsequential episode completely turns over our mutually exclusive understanding of myth and reason. As we stride toward Augustine's concept of life as something both written and yet-to-be-written, a careful look into the verbal act of creation in *Enuma Elis* will reveal a shared linguistic act of creation also present in the long Abrahamic tradition and the *Rule*.

Ahead of most of its homologs, the Ancient Near Eastern legend speaks of a time "when no destinies had been decreed" (*Enuma Elis* I.8). They have not yet been decided, that is. Leading to the crucial instant in which all fates are eventually set in stone, the genealogy laid down in "Tablet I" begins with a memorable cosmogonic scene well worth recounting,

When the heavens above did not exist,
And earth beneath had not come into being—
There was Apsu, the first in order, their begetter,
And demiurge Tiamat, who gave birth to them all;
They had mingled their waters together
Before meadow-land had coalesced and reed-bed was to be
    found—
When not one of the gods had been formed
Or had come into being, when no destinies had been decreed.
    (*Enuma Elis* I.1–9)

The mark of existence as we know it is the decretal of destinies. Deprived of the last verse, we could easily reduce the cosmogony to a customary myth-to-logos taxonomy, but appropriately highlighting this writing of fate reveals something crucial. As I will also wager in the case of the Abrahamic tradition, we may very well have gotten the myth-to-logos sequence wrong all this time. Let us have a look at the construction of myths in the birthplace of philosophy, Greece, so that we can understand why, from as early as the Mesopotamians, myth and logos might have not been as mutually exclusive as we thought. In fact, it can be argued that the myth starts with a moment of logos, that is, with a moment of foundational writing in the Book of Nature.

Francis MacDonald Cornford's 1912 notable *From Religion to Philosophy* presents a well-known taxonomy in which religion is advanced as the mother of philosophy. A starker lens was adopted by Wilhelm Nestle in his influential book from 1940, *From Myth to Logos* (*Vom Mythos zum Logos*). There, the history of the Ancient world, especially the Mediterranean, is neatly studied from the point of view of a transition from mythos to logos; from myth to reason. Although enlightening in many regards, Cornford's and Nestle's taxonomies involve a twofold limitation. First, they entail an irreversibly linear sense of progress in which an imperfect state of knowledge is ultimately replaced by a superior, fuller stage. Second, they presume both types of knowledge to be hermetically secluded.

Almost a century later, José Solana Dueso's innovative treatise from 2006, *De Logos a Physis: estudio sobre el Poema de Parménides* has presented a nuanced revision of this framework: What if the ancients did not so much abandon myth for reason, but nature for abstract thought? This interpretive lens emphasizes the

Pre-Socratics' predilection for deciphering the meaning of nature and does so while giving an account of the Parmenidean revolution. Additionally, it allows us to more finely differentiate between myth and reason as well as, more importantly, revealing the many instances of the intimate imbrication of the two. According to Solana's physis-to-logos model, the search for the absolute arche— beginning, principle, source. Led pioneer philosopher Thales of Miletus (624–545 BC) to posit that everything spawns out of water (Aristotle, *Metaphysics* 983.b6: 8–11, and 17–21). Many would soon join the discussion as they tried to uncover the foundation of everything in a variety of monistic principles: Anaximander (610– 456 BC) in the indefinite apeiron; Anaximenes (586–526 BC) in air; Pythagoras (570–495 BC) in numbers; Parmenides (515–450 BC) in being; Anaxagoras (500–428 BC) in the spermata or homoeomeries; Empedocles (494–434 BC) in the four elements; Democritus (460– 370 BC) in atoms. Less and less physical principles are formulated over time as Greek thought started prioritizing logos over physis. However, prioritizing does not mean abandoning. The physis-to-logos paradigm leaves room for the otherwise unconceivable combination of philosophical reason and the attribution of natural domains to many of the pantheon's gods to be explained. This is exactly where the primordial cosmos of *Enuma Elis* comes into full being as the world where the myth is, precisely, an act of logic. Centuries later, the Gospel of Saint John 1:14 will speak of Word— Logos—becoming flesh—Sarx.

As it does in the Greek pantheon, the even more ancient world of *Enuma Elis* is structured according to the natural domains of a variety of deities. Out of nothingness, Apsu, the Begetter, and Tiamat, the Demiurge, give birth to everything and everyone (*Enuma Elis* I.3–20). Thus are the first gods created, eventually leading to the triad of Anu—god of the sky—, Ea—god of water—, and Enlil—god of air and earth—, a god whose lineage is the ancestor trunk of all the current gods (IV.146).[3] Enlil, the Ruler, is the god

---

[3]Wilfred G. Lambert's *Babylonian Creation Myths* also provides some extraordinary insight into the complexity of the intertwining myths. Starting on page 180, the main takeaway point in this regard is that after the initial god-generating stage, reality and the heavens are divided into three sections with one corresponding to each one of the three major deities: Enlil, Ea, and Anu (whose names vary drastically across tablets, sources, and traditions). For a complete cosmogony, see Lambert's complete

watching over the Tablets of Destiny. Due to this very reason, Mesopotamians, Sumerians, Akkadians, Babylonians, Canaanites, and Assyrians worshipped Enlil—and many of his homologs—over all other deities. Since the syncretism of traditions could hinder the interpretation of the following passages, I ought to stress that, despite his privileged centrality in the canon, even Enlil appears under many names across the scripts.

There is indeed a breathtaking amount of regional and diachronic intermeshing of traditions surrounding the universe of *Enuma Elis*. While in some forms of the myth Marduk is tasked by Enlil with the care of humans, in others he goes to completely usurp Enlil's position in the cosmos. This is likely due to the fact that "enlil," a common noun and adjective not unlike the biblical "Elohim," also means "ruler" or "god." Often being named "Marduk, the enlil of the gods" (Tablet VII, vv.149) or Bel (Tablet VI, vv.70–81), it is not difficult to understand the propensity to syncretism, renaming, and alterations in the sequence (*Babylonian Creation Myths* 216). But what is important here is that the tradition of *Enuma Elis* places a major deity, pleonastically called Enlil, in charge of the very reason why we are talking about Mesopotamia as a bibliographical source to understand the evolution of coenobitism.

As the ruler of humanity, Enlil is intimately connected with all humans because, "he created the heavens and fashioned the earth" (Tablet VII, vv.135–6). The Greeks thought of the primigenial chaos as an abyssal gaping, disordered mouth of darkness. Out of disorder, the order of day and night, heaven and earth (Hesiod, *Theogony*, vv.115–36). The Bible, we will see, also reimagines the idea of a foundational crisis that is a division that is a word. A creational word. In the meantime, what is it about those Tablets of Destiny that took over Mesopotamian and Babylonian religion and thought?

The Tablets of Destiny or, more precisely, the Tablets of Destinies, contain every god's and every human's lives. Its prominence is proven by the fact that nearly all of the *Enuma Elis* tablets incorporate almost identical verses pertaining to the creation and bequeathal of the tablets (Tablet I, vv.154–8; Tablet II, vv.40–4;

---

reconstruction of the *Enuma Elis* cosmos in subsequent developments (*Babylonian Creation Myths* 198–9).

Tablet III, vv.43–8, and 100–6; Tablet VI, vv.70–81). The complexity
of the epos precipitated a myriad of translations, adaptations, and
interpretations across the ancient world, effectively resulting in the
same events being attributed to manifold gods depending on the hic
et nunc. Regardless, the events unfold thusly as Enlil-Marduk-Bel
convokes his fellows with a very purposeful goal in mind

> Bel seated the gods, his fathers, at the banquet
> In the lofty shrine which they had built for his dwelling,
> (Saying,) "This is Babylon, your fixed dwelling,
> Take your pleasure here! Sit down in joy!" The great gods sat
> down,
> Beer-mugs were set out and they sat at the banquet. After they
> had enjoyed themselves inside
> They held a service in awesome Esagil.
> The regulations and all the rules were confirmed:
> All the gods divided the stations of heaven and netherworld.
> The college of the Fifty great gods took their seats,
> The Seven gods of destinies were appointed to give decisions.
> (*Enuma Elis*, Tablet VI, vv.70–81)

The gods gather in symposium. Babylon, their predilect abode, sees
them confer and, in appropriate ancient divine conduct, rejoice in
pleasures. That is the precise moment in which chaos gives way
to order as humans got to know it. Reminiscent of the multiple
ontological separations found across the ancient cosmogonies, the
separation of heaven and netherworld establishes the final order
of the cosmos. In most of the correlated theogonies, it is Enlil the
Ruler—Ruler the Ruler—who commands the ultimate cosmic
caesura. Thus, he arrogates to himself the right to govern the now
orderly Earth. After writing down heaven, hell, and the fates of the
gods, the destiny of mankind must be engraved too:

> "I have delivered to you the rule of all the gods.
> You are indeed exalted, my spouse, you are renowned,
> Let your commands prevail over all the Anunnaki."
> She gave him the Tablet of Destinies and fastened it to his
> breast,
> (Saying) "Your order may not be changed; let the utterance of
> your mouth be firm." (*Enuma Elis*, Tablet I, vv.154–8)

The Tablet of Destinies rules over the Anunnaki, the fellowship of all other gods, as well as over humans. A passage from the oral to the written to the eternal indicates the sign of times to come as the Ancient Near Eastern cosmos is founded by a verbal act of creation in which destiny is inscribed onto seven tablets. All lives, even those of the gods, are therein recorded. In turn, the Tables of Destiny are the patrimony of Enlil, the supreme God of humanity.

The Ancient Near East is the home of power that "had no rival among the gods, his brothers" (Table I, vv.14–20).[4] Yet, how does the now supreme deity perpetuate such power? History is written by the vanquisher. Papyri, steles, stones, columns . . . . All can and have worked as consolidators of past events and governors of times to come. But what if one could scribe past, present, and future directly onto the human heart? A genotype of history of sorts, such inscription would imbue the ideal of biography with a radically new meaning. Concerned with the preservation of free will, Augustine will only go so far as to suggest that God is the author behind the syntax of existence. The gods of *Enuma Elis*, however, do not stop there. They author each one of the instants of each and every life; other gods' included.

The power of writing is transitive. Humans mimic the gods in their attempt at perpetuating words. Like most ancient myths, its ratification is linked to the confluence of cultic and legal texts. As a theogony, the cycle of *Enuma Elis* establishes the aforementioned *Code of Hammurabi*'s pioneering foundation. A code that embodies everything the present book is trying to capture: not only is it one

---

[4]The seizing of the pantheon is a tendency analogous to those studied by political theorists in the concentration—and potential dissolution—of power. Yehezkel Kaufmann build his work upon the foundational idea that monotheism is in direct, incommensurable opposition to the pagan idea of gods creating other gods and, in the case of *Enuma Elis*, gods determining the fates of other gods. Against that, "The mark of monotheism is not the concept of a god who is creator, eternal, benign, or even all-powerful; these notions are found everywhere in the pagan world. It is, rather, the idea of a god who is the source of all being, not subject to a cosmic order, and not emergent from a pre-existent realm; a god free of the limitations of magic and mythology. The high gods of primitive tribes do not embody this idea. To begin with, not all such gods are creators, which is to say that exaltedness does not involve temporal priority. Alongside of the high god there exists the universe of being, with all its forces. Moreover, those who are creators do not always create all things, nor do they always act alone" (*The Religion of Israel* 29–30).

of the oldest first-person texts, but also one of the most ancient rules ever written and one of the first texts whatsoever. Thus, Hammurabi's *Code* exposes the intimate connections between life-writing, regulating codes, and the theo-technological side of writing itself. On top of these traits, it preludes a type of pseudo-biographical writing characterized by the establishment of divine-human genealogies. Often aimed at legitimating a rule on earth, the deliberate filiation of the divine and human realms is established by Hammurabi through Hammurabi himself. By the means of intriguing synesthesia of adoration and usurpation, Hammurabi—Hammurabi the Enlil—does to Enlil what Enlil—Enlil the Enlil—did to Apsu. This move sets him out to occupy an intermediate position between heaven and earth. The codex's incipit manifests this self-proclaiming purpose:

> There was a time when exalted Anu, king of the Anunnaku,
> and Enlil, the lord of heaven and earth,
> who determines the destinies of the nation,
> determined that Marduk, the first son born to Ea,
> should govern as Enlil all the peoples of the world.
> They exalted him among the Igigi,
> and gave Babylon its illustrious name,
> and made it pre-eminent throughout the earth;
> with its foundations as secure as heaven and earth,
> they established for him an everlasting reign within it.
> It was then that Anu and Enlil ordained Hammurabi,
> a devout prince who fears the gods,
> to demonstrate justice within the land,
> to destroy evil and wickedness,
> to stop the mighty exploiting the weak,
> to rise like Shamash over the mass of humanity, illuminating the
>   land;
> they ordained me,
> to improve the welfare of my people.
> I am Hammurabi,
> Enlil's chosen shepherd. (*Hammurabi's Laws* 29, P1–P4)

Enlil's proper name as the supreme deity is as tautological as himself. As a common noun, Enlil simply means ruler. That is why Enlil can entrust Marduk with the command of the people. Marduk, in turn, asks Hammurabi to be his human-divine shepherd among humans. Hammurabi is the human ruler of the people; Marduk, is the divine ruler of the peoples; meanwhile, Enlil reigns supreme as the divine ruler of all divine rulers.[5] Enlil's power stems from his command of the Tablets of Destiny, which contain humanity's fate in its entirety. The only way for Hammurabi to legitimize his throne is by himself setting the fate of his own people in stone. Millenia before Walter Benjamin somewhat retrospectively reminded us that history is written by the victors, Hammurabi realizes that for him to become a more-than-human ruler, his rules will have to be set in stone in the lives of his subjects.[6] The story of life-writing has just begun.[7]

---

[5] "A common misunderstanding derived from this passage concerns the nature of the power given by Anu and Enlil. It is supreme power over the peoples. There is a title 'supreme ruler (Enlil) of the gods' current in Old Babylonian times, as will be shown, but this is not what could be applied to Marduk from the words quoted. Peoples and gods are two distinct groups which no ancient writer would have confused. Also, the passage states quite clearly that this authority was delegated. There is not a hint that Anu and Enlil abdicated when they decreed this appointment for Marduk. The grounds for this appointment are readily intelligible. When the city Babylon acquired political supremacy under Hammurabi, its god Marduk thereby triumphed—over the peoples. Thus, political reality was recognized in heaven by this promotion of Marduk to be ruler of the peoples. The authority of Anu and Enlil was not diminished, as is clear from their appointment of Hammurabi as king, though one would have expected Marduk, as ruling the peoples, to have done this. Following upon this opening sentence, the Prologue proceeds to list Hammurabi's connections with the major shrines, putting that of Enlil first, while Marduk's takes third place. The same state of affairs is presumed in the Epilogue: Enlil has assigned the human race to Hammurabi; Marduk directs him to shepherd it" (*Babylonian Creation Myths* 256).

[6] Not unlike Augustine, Walter Benjamin attributes great power to a concept of the present capable of sublating all passing, chronological temporality: "A historical materialist cannot do without the notion of a present which is not a transition, but in which time stands still and has come to a stop. For this notion defines the present in which he himself is writing history. Historicism gives the 'eternal' image of the past; historical materialism supplies a unique experience with the past. The historical materialist leaves it to others to be drained by the whore called 'Once upon a time' in historicism's bordello. He remains in control of his powers, man enough to blast open the continuum of history" (*Theses on the Philosophy of History* XVI). Courage is breaking chronology and giving way to the eternal present.

[7] Kaufmann has written extensively on the moral paradigm shift taking place as good and evil stop being pagan idols and star being perceived as existential attributes, the former becoming the closest to an affirmative definition of God's nature beyond the realm of negative theology: "The ethical moment was equally incapable of giving the

From Tablets to Books: Scripture of Life in the Abrahamic Tradition

Tanakh, Bible, and Quran are books of books. Not unlike the myths of *Enuma Elis*, they contain their fair share of laws, tablets, and commandments, as well as oral and written prophecies and traditions. Hence, it is just natural for readers to be tempted by the seductiveness of analogical pressure and assume that something like the prophet's words must be read as a mere translation of the Babylonian Tables of Destiny: "But you who forsake the Lord, who forget my holy mountain, who set a table for Fortune and fill cups of mixed wine for Destiny" (Isaiah 65:11). The revelation of a monotheistic God, however, changes everything. It transforms the meaning of fate, freedom, and language. Even writing itself undergoes a fundamental metamorphosis that demands a new explicative paradigm to be formulated.

The shared cultural substratum of the oecumene is not sufficient cause for monotheism to emerge. That is Yehezkel Kaufmann's argument in *The Religion of Israel, from Its Beginnings to the Babylonian Exile*. Regarding the syncretic nature of a pagan world where the Tables of Destinies rule over different civilizations and pantheons, Kaufmann argues that there is a nuclear, qualitative difference that must be considered in order to properly understand the true impact brought by the monotheistic revolution:

On the popular level, then, there was no essential difference between the pre-exilic Israelite and the pagan; both were children of the same culture. This view is here rejected in toto. We shall see that Israelite religion was an original creation of the people of Israel. It was absolutely different from anything the pagan world ever knew; its monotheistic world view had no antecedents in paganism. Nor was it a theological doctrine conceived and nurtured in limited circles or schools; nor a concept that finds

---

gods ultimate sovereignty. For morality is viewed by the pagan not as an expression of the sovereign will of the gods, but as part of the supernal order that governs the gods themselves. Morality, too, is, so to speak, part of nature, and its laws 'laws of nature'" (*The Religion of Israel* 38).

occasional expression in this or that passage or stratum of the Bible. It was the fundamental idea of a national culture, and informed every aspect of that culture from its very beginning. It received, of course, a legacy from the pagan age which preceded it, but the birth of Israelite religion was the death of paganism in Israel. (*The Religion of Israel* 2–3)

Theologically speaking, the new religion stipulates a worldview where there is a single, absolute source of power. God is not determined by other more highly deities or forces. There is not even a place for homologs and peers. Thousands of years later, theologians still debate a radical controversy that gained prominence, especially during the times of Saint Thomas Aquinas (1225–74), Duns Scotus (1265–1308), and William of Ockham (1285–1347), all of which engaged in the question regarding God's natural law and his ability, or lack thereof, to contravene the fundamental laws established by Himself. Can God's Will subvert or revise His own laws and His own necessary truths? Aquinas identifies God's moral laws as natural laws decreed by God for Creation and creatures to unfold according to His perfect Will. Ockham argues that God's power must be fully unrestricted as a requisite for it to be perfect; thus, not even the laws of nature decreed by God are seen as a condition imposed upon God, who could freely choose to turn His Will, even that theoretically contrary to the laws of nature, into laws of nature and morality. Scotus posits that the content of moral law is necessary *qua* natural law stemming from God. Ultimately, venturing into the realm of eternity demands that we enquire how free gods and God really are. This seemingly trifle question entails a fundamental distinction in ancient thought.

Due to the genealogical nature of the polytheistic pantheon, there is a plethora of instances in which pagan gods are subject to other gods' decisions regarding their fates. In the context of *Enuma Elis*, fate—the fate of humans and deities as decreed by the major gods—is the product of chaos and order embodied by Apsu and Tiamat. Gods, be it of thunder, air, or heaven, must abide by the laws of nature. Akin to the Greek gods and their often all-too-human tussles, not even Enlil's supremacy goes fully unquestioned. Gods are more powerful than humans or beasts, yet far from omnipotent, perfect, or infinite. They cannot be. Otherwise, how would we even start to conceive a polytheistic pantheon populated by any number of omnipotent, absolute deities? How would a multiplicity of absolutes operate? Gods, are born and, die often by their own hands or those of the parricidal tragedy. On the other hand, the biblical God is not the product of anyone or anything. He is absolute. Alpha and Omega.

The gods of polytheism are written in the preexisting grammar of existence; they may be the most powerful inhabitants of chaos and order, but they are nonetheless inhabitants. The monotheistic God incarnates all existence and the possibility of existence itself. Even the ferocious medieval dispute regarding God's ability to retract or alter the very laws of nature He created is one that departs from a radically different axiom: God is the source of all laws of nature. Whether He may be able to subvert the laws that He set in motion, or not, does not question the causal antecedence. From this point of view, a new theological taxonomy arises. All gods are writers in the Book of Nature. The polytheistic gods are written writers. The monotheistic God is the unwritten writer.

Poseidon or Ea can unchain aquatic events by writing the Book of Nature according to their will. They can add verses to the script of reality and do so more powerfully and skillfully than any human could dream of doing. Yet, their syntax and grammar have been given to them. The monotheistic God can, too, ignite floods and summon storms. Contrary to the polytheistic homologs, He could also choose for floods and storms to never have existed or even make them not mentally conceivable, a logical impossibility. He can narrate the epic of his people. Or elect for epic and people as concepts not ever to exist. The Aristotelian unmoved mover is, in fact, an unwritten writer. A grammar with no grammarian. A grammarian that is also the perfect syntax—the code of existence.

This distinction sheds new light on the very notion of freedom. Humans may or may not have free will. Since Augustine thought so despite ultimately believing in the insufficiency of the human agency before Grace, let us say we do. If we are free, we are free to do something—affirmative freedom—, or we are free from something—negative freedom. Consistently, gods would have incredibly potent wills and abilities to realize such will. They would be bound by fewer restrictions to enact their will. But God, the monotheistic God, is not just a quantitatively different entity with superior potency and power to execute his Free Will. He must be qualitatively incommensurable. Apart from infallibly enacting His

Will, He could have chosen for actions, freedom, and will never to have existed. The code of existence—the Book of Nature—is exactly the way He determined it because He so determined it. If there is free will, He created it. If there is rigorous determinism, He created it. The syntax of free will and determinism are different, but the fact is that there must be an ontological grammar, according to Augustine and most monotheistic thinkers. It could even be argued that a syntax of purely random clinamen would be, in fact, a syntax. Like the rare unloaded roulette, a perfect system of chance has a syntax that includes the design—dimensions, materials, gravity. Of the turret, the pockets, the ball tracks, the ball, the laws of gravity, the concept of color, that of vision, and even the existence of players themselves in their unique form. The strongest contribution of the Christian tradition is precisely the fact that God chooses to become human. He embraces mortality and chronology without ever surrendering His omnipotence and omniscience. By manifesting the eternal in human form, Christ renders the divine imitable to us. If everything is just mere chance, why do we write rules and precepts? Either they are absurd, or we are just operating in a Cartesian manner as a provisory moral system. A sort of Pascalian wager to save face in the plausible chance that we are indeed responsible for our acts.

The Tablets of the Law

The Torah is also the home of the most influential inscriptions in all of history. The Tablets of the Law, the first of two occurrences in the book of Exodus, are legated to humanity in a memorable passage of divine intervention through language, both spoken and written: "And he gave to Moses, when he had made an end of speaking with him upon Mount Sinai, the two tables of the testimony, tables of stone, written with the finger of God" (Exodus 31:18). This is a direct source of the manus Dei authoring a holy mandate. The monotheistic God does not just write the Book of Nature underlying all that exists and does not exist. He inscribes texts within texts, namely, the moral code of the Ten Commandments—the Tablets of Stone—engraved within the code of nature.

The absolute God of the Book does not only write the world; but also writes in the world. The book of Exodus provides surprisingly material, palpable details with respect to the nature of these in-the-world inscriptions by God Himself: "And Moses turned, and went down from the mountain with the two tables of the testimony in his hands, tables that were written on both sides; on the one side and on the other were they written. And the tables were the work of God, and the writing was the writing of God, graven upon the tables" (Exodus 32:15–16). The precise characterization of the divine language entering the world explains why thinkers such as Saint Augustine would spend so much time and effort trying to fathom the utterance of the words of creation, which in the case of Christianity were enriched by the developments of John's Gospel 1:1–18 and the idea of an incarnated Logos.[8] Before that, we hear

---

[8]While Augustine wonders how God's words of creation may have been uttered and how they might have flowed in or outside time itself, we cannot but relish the level of material detail found in the passage leading to the handing of the Tablets of the Law. For the law to be bestowed, God demands that the people build an appropriate receptacle which we know as the Ark of the Covenant: "They shall make an ark of acacia wood; two cubits and a half shall be its length, a cubit and a half its breadth, and a cubit and a half its height. And you shall overlay it with pure gold, within and without shall you overlay it, and you shall make upon it a molding of gold round about. And you shall cast four rings of gold for it and put them on its four feet, two rings on the one side of it, and two rings on the other side of it. You shall make poles of acacia wood, and overlay them with gold. And you shall put the poles into the rings on the sides of the ark, to carry the ark by them. The poles shall remain in the rings of the ark; they shall not be taken from it. And you shall put into the ark the testimony which I shall give you. Then you shall make a mercy seat of pure gold; two cubits and a half shall be its length, and a cubit and a half its breadth. And you shall make two cherubim of gold; of hammered work shall you make them, on the two ends of the mercy seat. Make one cherub on the one end, and one cherub on the other end; of one piece with the mercy seat shall you make the cherubim on its two ends. The cherubim shall spread out their wings above, overshadowing the mercy seat with their wings, their faces one to another; toward the mercy seat shall the faces of the cherubim be. And you shall put the mercy seat on the top of the ark; and in the ark you shall put the testimony that I shall give you. There I will meet with you, and from above the mercy seat, from between the two cherubim that are upon the ark of the testimony, I will speak with you of all that I will give you in commandment for the people of Israel" (Exodus 25:10–22). We know that the Tablets of the Law are in fact the Tablets of Stone; that is how important their material underpinning is. We are also told that the idolater's calf was made of molten gold. In the book of Daniel, the worshipped material gods learn a lesson after God sends the miraculous hand to write and admonish; the gentiles "drank wine, and praised the gods of gold and silver, bronze, iron, wood, and stone" (Daniel 5:4). Daniel 3 depicts a colorful, if bleak, portray of idolatry that has inspired Yehezkel Kaufmann to assert that,

of God writing tablets in His own hand. The content is one of beginnings, not endings. What is written is the covenant itself. A rule of life.

The paradigm shift—the move from determining the end to determining the beginning—caused by this undertaking is immeasurable and for sure the new axioms are incommensurable with those preceding them. The Tablets of Destiny from the pagan tradition were a relation of the events that were to occur to gods and humans alike; they are eschatological in the sense that they deal with the future and end of things. The Tablets of Destiny are, thus, chronological. The Tablets of the Law are the source of all human conduct that is good. They are a set of principles and beginnings, not ends. They come from God's eternity into temporality thanks to his generous gift in the form of engraved words. Instead of bringing a mere revision of a syncretic myth, the new tablets advance a radically new world of the covenant. However, having been sent the tablets to our chronological time resulted in what seems to be the end of most things human.

A prophetic but human hand, that of Moses, had received the tablets from God Himself. Not unlike Hammurabi's self-inscription in his laws, Moses feels the burden of responsibility as a direct depositary of the tablets. In Exodus 32, he beholds in desperation the disappointing scene of his community having demanded Aaron to forge an idol, the golden calf, a material sign of the people's impatience and ingratitude. He intercedes for his people in front of God, begging for mercy and promising to end the corruption of their customs, effectively buying them some time.[9] In turn, "As he

---

"The Bible conceives of idolatry as the belief that divine and magical powers inhere in certain natural or man-made objects and that man can activate these powers through fixed rituals. These objects, upon which magical rituals are performed, are 'the gods of the nations.' The Bible does not conceive the powers as personal beings who dwell in the idols; the idol is not a habitation of the god, it is the god himself" (*The Religion of Israel* 14).

[9]The aforementioned discussion involving Aquinas, Scotus, and Ockham regarding the reversibility of the natural laws finds a challenging turn in the Book of Exodus, whose account seems to present a God whose perfect plan nonetheless allows for jealousy, anger, wrath, and even recanting to take place: "And the Lord repented of the evil which he thought to do to his people" (Exodus 32:14). Was this change of mind of God—clearly an anthropomorphic expression—foretold by Himself in the original act of Creation?

drew near the camp, he saw the calf and the dancing. Then Moses' anger burned, and he threw the tablets down and broke them on the base of the mountain" (Exodus 32:19). The greatest gift so far in the history of mankind, a text coming directly from God's hands, has been squandered almost immediately after being received. Substituted by a forged, pointless idol, humanity has rejected the Word of God. Mercifully, God gives mankind a second chance; a chance to rewrite what God dictates, this time with the prophets as a conduit; the divine command asks Moses to "Cut two tables of stone like the first; and I will write upon the tables the words that were on the first tables, which you broke" (Exodus 34:1–10). The message leading to the promised land is still too great for a human hand to handle on its own. Over time, God's dictation will bear fruits and the stiff-necked people of ancient Israel will learn to cherish the established covenant.

The content of the tablets is an intricate matter linking the decalogues found in Exodus 20:2–17, Exodus 23:10–19, Exodus 34:11–26, and Deuteronomy 5:6–21. These fragments propose mostly homologous principles but their focus ranges from abstract, minimalistic rendition—"You shall have no other gods before me [. . .] You shall not kill" (Exodus 20:3–13)—to pronouncedly autochthonous formulations hardly susceptible to cultural extrapolation beyond the oecumene or even beyond the people of Israel—"The firstling of an ass you shall redeem with a lamb, or if you will not redeem it you shall break its neck. All the first-born of your sons you shall redeem. And none shall appear before me empty [. . .] You shall not boil a kid in its mother's milk" (Exodus 34:20–6).[10] The superposition of ritualistic practices, philosophical

---

[10]For the sake of proper contextualization, this is the most lauded formulation of the Commandments: "I am the Lord your God, who brought you out of the land of Egypt, out of the house of bondage. You shall have no other gods before me. You shall not make for yourself a graven image, or any likeness of anything that is in heaven above, or that is in the earth beneath, or that is in the water under the earth; you shall not bow down to them or serve them; for I the Lord your God am a jealous God, visiting the iniquity of the fathers upon the children to the third and the fourth generation of those who hate me, but showing steadfast love to thousands of those who love me and keep my commandments. You shall not take the name of the Lord your God in vain; for the Lord will not hold him guiltless who takes his name in vain. Remember the sabbath day, to keep it holy. Six days you shall labor,

principles, and political directions has not prevented the Ten Commandments from becoming a fundamental tenet of many civilizations and worldviews. Written and dictated by God Himself for the good of His people, the first set of life-writing in the Torah is also not the last case of divine interaction in the realm of language.

The Writing Is on the Wall

Aside from the bequeathal of the Tablets of the Law, the Old Testament encloses another marvelous episode of divine writing. The book of Daniel contains a memorable instance of the prophet's wisdom and humility. As Moses had acted as a conduit for God's Commandments, Daniel is asked to decipher a mysterious inscription that appeared as a result of the impiety manifested during the feast of King Belshazzar.

Nebuchadnezzar, a proud Chaldean king, had despoiled the Temple of Jerusalem, pillaging vessels and disrespecting the House of God. The ungrateful king, for all he ever had, was a gift from God, lost his humanity and was cast out of society. Instead of learning from his father's demise, his son—although other accounts make him the son of Nabonidus—King Belshazzar redoubled the haughty obstinacy of his father. One night, hoping to impress his guests during a banquet, Belshazzar persevered in his impiety by spurring them to inebriate themselves by means of the despoiled vessels taken from the Temple by his father. At that moment, "the fingers of a man's hand appeared and wrote on the plaster of the wall of the king's palace, opposite the lampstand; and the king

---

and do all your work; but the seventh day is a sabbath to the Lord your God; in it you shall not do any work, you, or your son, or your daughter, your manservant, or your maidservant, or your cattle, or the sojourner who is within your gates; for in six days the Lord made heaven and earth, the sea, and all that is in them, and rested the seventh day; therefore the Lord blessed the sabbath day and hallowed it. Honor your father and your mother, that your days may be long in the land which the Lord your God gives you. You shall not kill. You shall not commit adultery. You shall not steal. You shall not bear false witness against your neighbor. You shall not covet your neighbor's house; you shall not covet your neighbor's wife, or his manservant, or his maidservant, or his ox, or his ass, or anything that is your neighbor's" (Exodus 20:2–17).

saw the hand as it wrote. Then the king's color changed, and his thoughts alarmed him; his limbs gave way, and his knees knocked together" (Daniel 5:5–6). Always happy to defy the Lord of the Temple whose vessels he had demeaned, Belshazzar is nonetheless flustered; the stupefying nature of the witness events made him call the depositaries of pagan knowledge, from enchanters to diviners, to have the mysterious inscription deciphered and explained. As usual, when coming from an opulent figure that has turned his back to the spiritual world, all he has to offer in return is the material munificence of lavishness and worldly fame "Whoever reads this writing, and shows me its interpretation, shall be clothed with purple, and have a chain of gold about his neck, and shall be the third ruler in the kingdom" (Daniel 5:7–9). None of them could produce a working interpretation. Then, the prophetic, scholarly, almost Freudian abilities of Daniel are suggested as a potential solution to the enigma.

The prophet is characterized as someone who can read the divine text of the world. The king, in turn, admits: "Now the wise men, the enchanters, have been brought in before me to read this writing and make known to me its interpretation; but they could not show the interpretation of the matter. But I have heard that you can give interpretations and solve problems" (Daniel 5:15–16). Interpreting is defined here in a strikingly similar manner to that of Saint Augustine in *The Teacher*; Augustine defines interpretation as finding love in the tapestry of nature. In the book of Daniel, a prophet is an interpreter capable of devising the pedagogical nature of all of God's signs. Munificently, Daniel rejects the king's offerings but acquiesces to the petition and proceeds to interpret the signs. What he finds is the rebellion and impiety of the Chaldean rulers followed by the denial to learn from past and present mistakes.[11]

---

[11] The king's sin is a combination of pride, impiety, rebelliousness, and idolatry: "And you his son, Belshaz'zar, have not humbled your heart, though you knew all this, but you have lifted up yourself against the Lord of heaven; and the vessels of his house have been brought in before you, and you and your lords, your wives, and your concubines have drunk wine from them; and you have praised the gods of silver and gold, of bronze, iron, wood, and stone, which do not see or hear or know, but the God in whose hand is your breath, and whose are all your ways, you have not honored" (Daniel 5:22–3). This exegesis reinforces the scholarly notion that the Ten Commandments are interlaced to the point of being interdependent; breaking one is

The irreverence of the vain king forced God to take part, and "Then from his presence the hand was sent, and this writing was inscribed" (Daniel 5:24).[12] This second episode of divine writing, not of but in the Book of Nature, manifests the power attributed to words by the religions of the Book. In some extraordinary cases, God Himself has to intervene through the use of language. The dictation of the Ten Commandments and the writing on the wall will not be the last divine utterances to grace the biblical text.[13]

---

more often than not followed by the violation of several other commandments. That might be the reason why the New Testament decants the multiplicity of principles into a simple, universal one that concerns both divine and temporal affairs: "'you shall love the Lord your God with all your heart, and with all your soul, and with all your mind, and with all your strength.' The second is this, 'You shall love your neighbor as yourself.' There is no other commandment greater than these" (Mark 12:30–1).

[12]The exact content of the writing on the wall is then legated. The phrasing is just remarkable: "And this is the writing that was inscribed: Mene, Mene, Tekel, and Parsin. This is the interpretation of the matter: Mene, God has numbered the days of your kingdom and brought it to an end; Tekel, you have been weighed in the balances and found wanting; Peres, your kingdom is divided and given to the Medes and Persians" (Daniel 3:25–8). Despite the inconsistencies regarding Belshazzar's genealogy, the recited events are broadly related to the eventual fall of Babylon.

[13]The Augustinian Rule might be the final destination of this genealogy of divine writing, but no account of Abrahamic literature would be complete without at least glossing over one of the most fascinating manifestations of the divine syntax. In an astonishing, yet consistent turn of events, many Islamic scholars speak of the creational acts of God via the Absolute Pen. One of the key sources is the Book of Decrees, but there are explicit references to the motifs of the tablets of destiny and the writing of Creation in Quran 7:145: "We inscribed everything for him in the Tablets which taught and explained everything, saying, 'Hold on to them firmly and urge your people to hold fast to their excellent teachings. I will show you the end of those who rebel.'" According to the Muslim account, the Tablets of the Old Testament are retrieved and reinstated; the Islamic retelling of the veterotestamentary narration states: "On his return to his people, angry and aggrieved, Moses said, 'How foul and evil is what you have done in my absence! Were you so keen to bring your Lord's judgement forward?' He threw the tablets down and seized his brother by the hair, pulling him towards him. Aaron said, 'Son of my mother, these people overpowered me! They almost killed me! Do not give my enemies reason to rejoice! Do not include me with these evildoers!'" (Quran 7:150). And then, "When Moses' anger abated, he picked up the Tablets, on which were inscribed guidance and mercy for those who stood in awe of their Lord" (Quran 7:154). A most fascinating motif is also recovered when we read that after the Absolute Pen has written all of Creation, its scribing no new names may be added to the Book. Conversely, Revelation 20, states that no changes can be made to the prophecy book, Revelation itself, but there is a

Tablet of the Heart

The Christian worldview furnishing Augustine's philosophy will take the beginning-oriented approach from the Torah and combine it with the eschatological, ending-oriented Four Last Things present in Revelation. A most influential source during this transitional period is also one of the most preeminent collections of wisdom literature, the words of Solomon in the book of Proverbs.[14]

---

door open to adding our names to the Book of Life. A key source in this exploration is *Divine Will and Predestination in the Light of the Qur'an and Sunnah*, by Dr. 'Umar S. al-Ashqar.

[14]One could certainly argue that different schools of Jewish thought have defined moral agency in ways compatible with a broad sense of predestination. Flavius Josephus (AD 37–100), whose work I considered extensively in the previous volume, *On Hellenism, Judaism, Individualism, and Early Christian Theories of the Subject*, recollects that, "At this time there were three sects among the Jews, who had different opinions concerning human actions. The one was called the sect of the Pharisees; another the sect of the Sadducees; and the other the sect of the Essens. Now for the Pharisees, they say that some actions, but not all are the work of fate: and some of them are in our own power; and that they are liable to fate, but are not caused by fate. But the sect of the Essens affirm, that fate governs all things; and that nothing befalls men but what is according to its determination. And for the Sadducees, they take away fate; and say there is no such thing; and that the events of human affairs are not at its disposal: but they suppose that all our actions are in our own power; so that we are our selves the causes of what is good, and receive what is evil from our own folly" (*Antiquities of the Jews*, Book XIII, Chapter 5.9). This is complemented by a memorable fragment of his book on the war: "But then as to the two other orders at first mentioned, the Pharisees are those who are esteemed most skilful in the exact explication of their laws, and introduce the first sect. These ascribe all to fate [or providence], and to God, and yet allow, that to act what is right, or the contrary, is principally in the power of men; although fate does co-operate in every action. They say that all souls are incorruptible, but that the souls of good men only are removed into other bodies, but that the souls of bad men are subject to eternal punishment. But the Sadducees are those that compose the second order, and take away fate entirely, and suppose that God is not concerned in our doing or not doing what is evil; and they say, that to act what is good, or what is evil, is at men's own choice, and that the one or the other belongs so to every one, that they may act as they please. They also take away the belief of the immortal duration of the soul, and the punishments and rewards in Hades. Moreover, the Pharisees are friendly to one another, and are for the exercise of concord, and regard for the public; but the behaviour of the Sadducees one towards another is in some degree wild, and their conversation with those that are of their own party is as barbarous as if they were

The proverbs of Solomon establish a direct, causal connection between fear of God and wisdom—the metuentes are the wise. Against the esotericism and covertness of many ancient cults for which the truth was restricted patrimony of the chosen few, the Jewish passion for knowledge founds a school of thought that would be relished by kabbalists and mystics: "The fear of the Lord is the beginning of knowledge; fools despise wisdom and instruction" (Proverbs 1:7). After having instituted the monotheistic God as the definitive source of enlightenment, a phenomenal veer takes place concerning the manifestation of the divine through language in this world:

> My son, do not forget my teaching,
> but let your heart keep my commandments;
> for length of days and years of life
> and abundant welfare will they give you.
> Let not loyalty and faithfulness forsake you;
> bind them about your neck,
> write them on the tablet of your heart.
> So you will find favor and good repute
> in the sight of God and man. (Proverbs 3:1–5)

The strong focus on the commandments has evolved subtly but profoundly, for the tablet is not anymore seen only as the banner of the national covenant, but also as a standard that must be inscribed in each one of the members' hearts. Commandment, tablet, and heart are three essential concepts that make sense of this transcendental development taking place in Proverbs 3.

Commandment. The first term germane to our discussion term in Proverbs 3:1 is no other than *torah* (Strong, *Exhaustive Concordance of the Bible* 8451), an utterly important word. The homonymous book is a book of commandments that contains books of commandments, so the Jewish text and the corresponding parts of the Old Testament borrow their name from this precise concept, which is frequently translated as teaching, direction, guidance, law, commandment, precept, or rule. To make matters

---

strangers to them. And this is what I had to say concerning the philosophic sects among the Jews" (*Of the War*, Book II, Chapter 8.14).

even more enthralling, *torah*—a beautiful coalescence of wisdom and law—adopts this time a pedagogical sense of command as a lesson while its mirror concept, *mitsvah* (Strong 4687), takes on the more legalistic sense of commandment as an obligation, as law.

In a meaningful turn of events, Saint Jerome's Vulgate opts for *praecepta* and *legis* as his own, influential versions of these capital taxa. Over time, even though Saint Augustine mostly used an intermediate text to that of the Vetus Latina and the Vulgate, the main document we use when studying his monastic contributions is, precisely, a *praeceptum*, a book of precepts that we call the *Rule*. His monastic rule, *praeceptum*, employs both *praecepta* and *lex* in several occasions. Meaningfully, Augustine uses the term *lex* at the end of the main manuscript, the *Praeceptum* (VIII.1), as the saint formally restricts its use to the law of the Old Covenant, preferring instead the notion of *praeceptum* as his own version of the existential rule of the Christian life. Moreover, the law is presented as a former state which has been superseded by the new stage of living in freedom under Grace (*Praeceptum* VIII.1). Naturally, this transition is facilitated by the presence of the Hebrew term for favor or grace, *chen* (Strong, *The Exhaustive Concordance of the Bible* 2580). The fourth versicle speaks of finding "favor and good repute in the sight of God and man," that is "invenies gratiam, et disciplinam bonam, coram Deo et hominibus" (Proverbs 3:4). Even though the proverb expects humans to act wisely, the notion of divine favor as Grace would eventually become a self-sufficient—exclusive, even—force in the Augustinian theory of salvation. In due course, the path taken by the proverb and those verses in Revelation 20 would torment an aging Augustine's fragile relationship with the soteriology of deeds versus Grace. The solution was always present in the following verses in Proverbs 3.

Tablet. The first and second versions of the Ten Commandments bestowed to the Jewish people were handed, then dictated to Moses atop Mount Sinai. The tablets were not just tablets, they were Tablets of Stone, for their material is as important as the metonymies and metaphors constructed around Saint Peter's onomastics would be for the incipient Christian world. As the Essenes had found refuge in the crevices and clefts of the rocky deserts, the two covenants are built on solid ground. The tablets are made of robust stone. Yet, Proverbs 3:3 finds a completely different foundation for the commandments leading to fertile fear and wisdom with God. The precepts of the law are to find a most unique abode: "Let not loyalty and faithfulness forsake you; bind them about your neck, write them on the tablet of your heart," also "Misericordia et veritas te non deserant; circumda eas gutturi tuo, et describe in tabulis cordis tui" (Proverbs 3:3). The law shall accompany each one of us in the shape of a holy collar of wisdom. Not just that, it must also be inscribed on the very heart of the bearer. The unheralded fabric of this new commandment does, however, find a magnificent echo in another text of wisdom, the book of Ezekiel. A decisive episode in the prophet's account sees God, a patient God, giving humanity yet another chance and renewing the bonds that humanity often fails to cherish: "A new heart I will give you, and a new spirit I will put within you; and I will take out of your flesh the heart of stone and give you a heart of flesh" (Ezekiel 36:26; also 11:19). The commandments have found a new cardiac residence. The heart itself is not made of stone anymore. The flesh of the grateful heart welcomes and animates the law.

Heart. The commandments are to be kept by no other custodian than the human heart. In fact, the only path to a long, good life is writing those precepts in the primary driver of corporal life. "My son, do not forget my teaching, but let your heart keep my commandments [. . .] write them on the tablet of your heart" (Proverbs 3:1–3). The endeavor we are called to undertake is one of harboring and cherishing the teachings, "praecepta mea cor tuum custodiat"; a recurring word in the Scripture, *leb* (Strong 3820), embodies the inner man, the heart, and the force inside every one of us. Moreover, Proverbs 3:5 opens the door to another crucial element of the Augustinian outlook,

> Trust in the Lord with all your heart,
> and do not rely on your own insight.
> In all your ways acknowledge him,
> and he will make straight your paths.
> Be not wise in your own eyes;
> fear the Lord, and turn away from evil. (Proverbs 3:5–7)

Mankind's freedom has been squandered and subsequently maimed by mankind itself. Even though free will is still there, the ability to fully embrace it is impaired in the hearts of the massa damnata. As opposed to the Ancient Near Eastern cosmology, the tables of the biblical covenant tell us that life being written does not deprive us of free will but ascribes us the moral responsibility unchained in the Tree of Knowledge of Good and Evil. The syntax of the world has been designed by the grammarian architect, but the sentences of each heart's life are yet to be written. Yet, how are humans to write our own lives in good faith if we are also reminded not to rely on our own insight? Grace, Augustine's solution to the conundrum, would eventually grant him the title of *Doctor gratiae*, effectively becoming the first Doctor of the Church to receive a special title. By incorporating Grace, Augustine opens a promising but arduous door to solving the tension between determinism and indeterminism, between necessity and freedom. Even though most translations favor "favor" as a translation of *chen*, Augustine will find a strong foundation for the idea of Grace. Grace as a divine favor to be supplemented with the sane use of free will is the promised escape route out of the massa damnata. However, the prophet exhorts us to trust God alone in this endeavor. And trusting God is trusting our fellows above our fallible insight, for it is ultimately worthless to be wise in your own eyes. As we walk our hearts back to the indelible covenant, human finitude and insufficiency after the Fall ought to inspire us to found a human koinonia. A society of love.

Imitable

The advent of Jesus Christ changes everything. The absolute God that entrusted Moses with the Tablets of Stone and admonished the great prophets to embrace the commandments in the spirited flesh of our living hearts had always known that there would be a day when the Word would have to become flesh. The Incarnation ensuing the period of advent signals a paradigm shift in so far as the human-divine relationship. The monotheistic God had never been the Spinozian or Epicurean indifferent master in the distance, but the level of proximity achieved by the divine decision of becoming man takes to a completely different level from the preceding levels of interactions by the means of language, prophets, or even direct intervention. Humans partake in the divine nature of creation to the point that when God created man, "he made him in the likeness of God" (Genesis 5:1). The Incarnation sheds a penetrating light onto and into the notion of the imago Dei: "In the beginning was the

Word, and the Word was with God, and the Word was God [. . .] And the Word became flesh and dwelt among us, full of grace and truth; we have beheld his glory, glory as of the only Son from the Father" (John 1:1–14). It is God Himself that chooses to become human. He does not need to do it, yet He does.

The Incarnation has radical consequences. The Tablets of Stone, the Ten Commandments, was bestowed to mankind as the faultless textbook of life. The Scripture itself—the book containing the books—was. Nevertheless, a perfect book, a perfect rule, is only as good as its following. Mankind, we know, failed and fails over and over again. We disappoint, betray, beguile, and squander the most wondrous gifts in a perennial circle of ungrateful self-destruction. The best teachers, however, are not just those who share—or even compose—the best textbook. They become their teaching, for teaching the definitive lesson and being the definitive lesson can be vastly different things. God's plan was always the same and the Tablets of Stone are no less true thereafter, but the Incarnation unites humans and laws in a qualitatively different manner: humans are not anymore asked to do as God says but to do as He does. As He is. The rule is not followed but imitated.

To be fair, the era of the prophets had regaled humanity with extraordinary models of conduct. Saints, too, will help to inspire and guide mankind as we face new challenges every day of this mortal chronology of ours. The tablets were already the perfect rule. Yet, following the perfect rule and imitating a virtuous follower of the rule involve different operations when compared to imitating the ruler directly. The rule of the Ten Commandments is written, and I might understand it or not; I might follow it or not; I might follow it correctly or not. When the lives of prophets and saints are lived, I might understand them or not; I might imitate them or not; I might imitate them correctly or not. The coming of Jesus Christ, however, yields an incommensurable scenario. The Ruler becomes the rule according to the parameters of the rule's understanding. Christians are not asked to understand and abide by the law; they are called to love and imitate human life. That, we can do. It is certainly the least ordinary of human lives, but it is also—it had to be—an ordinary human life that everyone can learn to imitate. The teacher does not just impart the most perfect of truths. He does not just deliver the most unsurpassable course materials. He leads by example. The mystery of the Incarnation renders the law imitable.

The Augustinian theory of the teacher ultimately leads to recognizing that, since all truth must come from divine sources, all teaching is but a process of discovery trough which each soul unveils—aletheia as revealing truth, not veritas in the sense of correspondence—the truth that was always inside. A truth we already knew, Christ reminds us:

> And as he was setting out on his journey, a man ran up and knelt before him, and asked him, "Good Teacher, what must I do to inherit eternal life?" And Jesus said to him, "Why do you call me good? No one is good but God alone. You know the commandments: 'Do not kill, Do not commit adultery, Do not steal, Do not bear false witness, Do not defraud, Honor your father and mother.'" And he said to him, "Teacher, all these I have observed from my youth." (Mark 10:17–20)

The good teacher does not just tell the truth, He is the very truth he teaches. Prior to Him, there had been immaculate laws and commendable followers of those laws. In Him and with Him, Christ is the unsurpassable embodiment of a human life lived in perfect accordance with the spirit of the law. The invaluable tradition of Jewish wisdom yields the keenest students of the law. Christ's embodiment of the law departs from an implied understanding and study of that law so that His human fellows can just do as the teacher does and live as the teacher, an infallible one, lives. The rule of the commandment is not followed anymore. It is imitable and, hopefully, imitated.

Following a rule is imitating the rule. From here onwards, Christian soteriology does not need to imagine heaven or the perfect life. The vita Christi is already the final destination. An infallible roadmap to living the perfect life without the need to involve neither fantasy nor speculation. There is, of course, a naturally emerging caveat: How do we apply the imitation of Christ's life if we are neither infallible, divine, nor God Himself? We could try to be born to Mary and Joseph in Bethlehem in the age of Tiberius. This would be Pierre Menard's approach. Maybe too easy for one. But we could also find love in everything we do. This is what Augustine calls interpretation. Living a life of pure love in everything we do and are. We do not live a Christian life. We are Christian life. Living not in accordance, but in imitation of the optimal, unimprovable of the commandments as we try to transcend human chronology and reach eternity. Augustine's *Rule* is a history of mankind overcoming the chronology of mortality with the help of mortality. To reach the absolute time of eternity—a time of absolute love—, the *Rule* makes the imitation of Christ not just feasible, but a bit less unlikely. The history of scriptural writing concludes when the names of those who have imitated the Lord finally are found in the Book of Life. The Scripture—which Augustine liked to call the Book or Skin of Heaven—is then embellished with the names of the meek and the humble: "Nevertheless do not rejoice in this, that the spirits are subject to you; but rejoice that your names are written in heaven" (Luke 10:20).

5

Soteriology of Imitation

Soteriology of Imitation

The Incarnation of God renders the rule not just obeyable, but also imitable. In accordance with this revolution, the New Testament produces a renewed theory of salvation. A soteriology of imitation. As Augustine strives toward the salvation in the Body of Christ, a new temple—body, house, monastery—is erected: "Live then, all of you, in harmony and concord; honour God mutually in each other; you have become His temples" (*Praeceptum* I.8).[1] The temple of the body is the humble abode for the new, imitable law.

Whereas there is no salient equivalent in the Old Testament, the concept of imitation bursts forth as an integral pillar of the Pauline Epistles; specifically, 1 Corinthians 4:16, 11:1; Ephesians 5:1; 1 Thessalonians 1:6, 2:14; Hebrews 6:12, 13:7. Meaningfully, the words *mimétés* (imitator, follower) and *mimeomai* (to imitate, to follow) proliferate in an extremely specific and telling part of the Scripture. Why? Because the epistles are the bridge of imitation that connects the first following of the Gospels' teachings in Acts of the Apostles to the trying tests of Revelation. By practicing imitation—a new form of following a rule—the apostles embraced Christ's Commandments and built a first community to inaugurate the New Covenant, the apostolic koinonia of Jerusalem. Having proven to the world that man can do a fair job at imitating Christ, the letters are the New Testament's tool to promulgate that imitation is the path

---

[1] "Omnes ergo unianimiter et concorditer uiuite, et honorate in uobis inuicem deum cuius templa facti estis" (*Praeceptum* I.8)

to follow. The First Epistle to the Corinthians summarizes the new principle of rule-following as rule-imitation: "Be imitators of me, as I am of Christ" (1 Corinthians 11:1). In turn, Philippians exhorts the imitators to "symmimetai mou," that is, to imitate the apostle and to "conduct themselves according to the model you have in us" (3:17–19). The concept used to describe this model is no other than "typon," and a type is exactly what imitation is built upon. Complementarily, Ephesians 5 synthetizes these efforts to communicate the recently discovered imitability—versus the former obeyability—of the law while also opening the path to a new soteriology:

> Therefore be imitators of God, as beloved children. And walk in love, as Christ loved us and gave himself up for us, a fragrant offering and sacrifice to God. But immorality and all impurity or covetousness must not even be named among you, as is fitting among saints. Let there be no filthiness, nor silly talk, nor levity, which are not fitting; but instead let there be thanksgiving. Be sure of this, that no immoral or impure man, or one who is covetous (that is, an idolater), has any inheritance in the kingdom of Christ and of God. (Ephesians 5:1–5)

The oration passage embodies the spirit of the new relationship with the law that calls all to become "imitators of God" living a life of love. The continuation of the sacrificial discourse presents a subtle but pivotal transformation as the commandments adopt the personal tone preluded by the wisdom of the book of Proverbs. It is again in Philippians where a name to the new community leading to the kingdom is finally given: "our commonwealth is in heaven, and from it we await a Savior, the Lord Jesus Christ, who will change our lowly body to be like his glorious body, by the power which enables him even to subject all things to himself" (3:20–1). Imitation of Christ—letting our bodies become His Body—as a new form of citizenship which leads to a new paradigm of soteriological thought. The soteriology of imitation leads to an eschatology of imitation.

Eschatology of Imitation

A new life will see the light of day—an eternal day with no night—when the first things have passed away (Revelation 21:1–8). This is the life of freedom under Grace that Augustine wants for his brothers and sisters. A new life in the mystical city of New Jerusalem, the holy, eternal city promised in the book of Revelation:

> Then I saw a new heaven and a new earth; for the first heaven and the first earth had passed away, and the sea was no more. And I saw the holy city, new Jerusalem, coming down out of heaven from God, prepared as a bride adorned for her husband; and I heard a great voice from the throne saying, "Behold, the dwelling of God is with men. He will dwell with them, and they shall be his people, and God himself will be with them; he will wipe away every tear from their eyes, and death shall be no more, neither shall there be mourning nor crying nor pain any more, for the former things have passed away." And he who sat upon the throne said, "Behold, I make all things new." Also he said, "Write this, for these words are trustworthy and true." And he said to me, "It is done! I am the Alpha and the Omega, the beginning and the end. To the thirsty I will give water without price from the fountain of the water of life. He who conquers shall have this heritage, and I will be his God and he shall be my son. But as for the cowardly, the faithless, the polluted, as for murderers, fornicators, sorcerers, idolaters, and all liars, their lot shall be in the lake that burns with fire and brimstone, which is the second death." (Revelation 21:1–8)

The neotestamentary soteriology of imitation promises the inheritance of the kingdom to those who follow—who imitate—the rule. A culmination of its role as the Body of Christ, the city reunites itself fully as the mystical Bride of God. There is no rupture; no separation; no misplaced love. One language: the language of love partially unearthed while on Earth by Augustine's exegetical methodology of interpretation. One love; the same preached by Augustine's *Rule* as the only certain path toward God while we inhabit this mortal chronology of ours. One scroll of eternal onomasticon to chant the names of those that will overcome the second, final death.

There is a scroll and there is a throne. The throne of Revelation 20:11 is the seat of judgment where the last words will be heard, "standing before the throne, and books were opened. Also another book was opened, which is the book of life. And the dead were judged by what was written in the books, by what they had done" (Revelation 20:12). A judgment *kata ta erga auton*—according to the deeds of them. The onomasticon, a scroll revealed to be none other than the "Lamb's Book of Life" that will judge all according to our deeds (Revelation 21:27).[2] After the first things have passed away, our lives will too be collated and judged by looking at the book. "Behold, I am coming soon, bringing my recompense, to repay every one for what he has done. I am the Alpha and the Omega, the first and the last, the beginning and the end" (Revelation 22:12–13). In view of this, will our names be there when it really matters?

Imitating the rule is not a hollow language game. There is a criterion of truth. A mystical one, to be sure. Having been handed the perfect life written for us in the unsurpassable example of the vita Christi, all that is left is for the Judge to collate the Son's perfect biography and our imitation thereof. The Book of Life will be read aloud; chronology will end and those whose life has mirrored that of the Son will bear His Name on their foreheads. Their names will be found in the Book of Life and they will no longer need to imitate the Lord, for they will sit right next to Him.

Great names will be read aloud for eternity to hear. A long time ago, Moses himself had relinquished his own name, using it as moral currency when he implored God to give Israel a second chance after the disappointing return to idolatry and the destruction

---

[2]In the previous volume, I characterized the end goal of the present endeavor. Whereas the first book describes the egalitarian koinon to be established by ancient, Second Temple, and early Christian coenobites, I have here described the reasoning leading to the installation of one such model of citizenship based on affirmative freedom and negative subjectivity. As I said, the key moment in this development is the internalization of the Temple, which becomes temple of the heart in the hands of the Essenes and other Second Temple Jews. From there, the new form of social body culminates in the idea of the Body of Christ: "I saw no temple in the city, for its temple is the Lord God the Almighty and the Lamb. And the city has no need of sun or moon to shine upon it, for the glory of God is its light, and its lamp is the Lamb. By its light shall the nations walk; and the kings of the earth shall bring their glory into it, and its gates shall never be shut by day—and there shall be no night there; they shall bring into it the glory and the honor of the nations. But nothing unclean shall enter it, nor any one who practices abomination or falsehood, but only those who are written in the Lamb's book of life" (Revelation 21:22–7). Why, then, care about the body in such a careful manner as that found in Augustine's *Rule* and most monastic constitutions? Because, per 1 Corinthians 6:19, our bodies are the new temple, the new house of imitation and love.

of the first Tablets of the Commandments: "'if thou wilt forgive their sin—and if not, blot me, I pray thee, out of thy book which thou hast written.' But the Lord said to Moses, 'Whoever has sinned against me, him will I blot out of my book'" (Exodus 32:30–4). If sin involves having our name blotted out of the divine registry, does that mean that virtue can lead to our name being inscribed? If that were the case, we might be tempted to go ahead and simply scribble our initials when nobody is looking at the Book of Life. Inebriated in pride, some will even try to do that in plain sight. However, nobody other than God can inscribe the names. The prophecy of Revelation is sealed and protected, as the Book of Life is: "I warn every one who hears the words of the prophecy of this book: if any one adds to them, God will add to him the plagues described in this book, and if any one takes away from the words of the book of this prophecy, God will take away his share in the tree of life and in the holy city, which are described in this book" (Revelation 22:18–19). The book of Revelation reveals the Book of Life which, in turn, reveals the Book of Creation. Many will come and try to inscribe their name on them. Mercifully, we were warned that people would come praising their own names and claiming the throne of God for themselves (2 Thessalonians 2:4). To guard us and the gleaming city of New Jerusalem against the usurpers, the eschatology of imitation establishes a brilliant failsafe; since it is the names of the onomasticon that reveal the fate of each one of us, God made the sign of those names visible. Impossible to miss, in fact, for the mark of salvation—the name of God—or damnation—the name of the beast—is inscribed on our very foreheads. The outcome of our imitative life can be measured by looking at ourselves in the mirror. Will our skin say the name of the beast or will it chant the name of God? Before those bearing the saving name of God on their foreheads are selected, the souls of those stained by the name of the beast are exposed and condemned:

> I saw the souls of those who had been beheaded for their testimony to Jesus and for the word of God, and who had not worshiped the beast or its image and had not received its mark on their foreheads or their hands. They came to life, and reigned with Christ a thousand years. The rest of the dead did not come to life until the thousand years were ended. This is the first resurrection. Blessed and holy is he who shares in the first

resurrection! Over such the second death has no power, but they shall be priests of God and of Christ, and they shall reign with him a thousand years. (Revelation 20:4–6)

Moses offered to have his name blotted out from the divine onomasticon. Christ, the Judge, examines each and every forehead looking for names. Like cattle, those exhibiting the name of the beast will take the left turn; later, we will see, those displaying God's very name on their skin taking the right turn to heaven. Augustine's exegesis of the Gospel of John interprets this omen by identifying the prideful opponent and his followers as those who worship their own name: "'He who speaks on his own seeks his own glory.' This will be that one who is called the Antichrist, 'exalting himself,' as the Apostle says, 'above all that is called God and that is worshipped'" (*Tractates on the Gospel of John* XXIX.8). Conversely, many of those being judged according to their deeds will bear the sign of the Lamb. The right turn guides them to finally seeing the face of a God that had chosen to conceal His face even from the prophet Moses on Mount Sinai, an occasion of old where God had chosen to turn His back instead.[3] When Moses and his people were given a second chance, he receives a peculiar instruction: "while my glory passes by I will put you in a cleft of the rock, and I will cover you with my hand until I have passed by; then I will take away my hand, and you shall see my back; but my face shall not be seen" (Exodus 33:22–3). The light coming from the face had always remained too beautiful, too true, too loving for any humans to even survive the exposure. That is why God gave mankind mortality and chronology, an appropriately scaled learning curve guided by a loving teacher. Even though the illumination by the face is well known, we tend to omit the corollary to that vision, which is the fact that those

---

[3]The mirror as means of—truncated—knowledge is found in both the Pauline Epistles and the work of Wittgenstein: "For now we see in a mirror dimly, but then face to face. Now I know in part; then I shall understand fully, even as I have been fully understood" (1 Corinthians 13:12). And, in the case of the Austrian philosopher, "Think of the recognition of facial expressions. Or of the description of facial expressions—which does not consist in giving the measurements of the face. Think, too, how one can imitate a man's face without seeing one's own in a mirror" (*Philosophical Investigations* §285). A mirror might not reflect it all, but it is better than nothing.

who finally are allowed to see God's face are also the ones to bear His Name on their foreheads, that is, the good imitators of Christ: "they shall see his face, and his name shall be on their foreheads. And night shall be no more; they need no light of lamp or sun, for the Lord God will be their light, and they shall reign for ever and ever" (Revelation 22:4–5). As Saint Augustine liked to refer to the Scripture as the Skin of Heaven, New Jerusalem is the city of those with God's Name written on the book of the human skin.

A Mirror of Eternity

The divine vision of God's face has been a fruitful motif that mystical traditions across the globe were delighted to embrace. Augustine embraces the mystical death of the old self—self-effacement that results in affirmative freedom—when he implores God to take what is left of this mortal body and trade it for a glimpse at the absolute, perennial light: "Hide not Thy face from me: let me die so that I may see it, lest I die" (*Confessions* I.5). That instant of illumination allows us to infer a system in the workings of the Last Judgment. We know of the Judgment's procedures and the importance of deeds, but the extent of free will's participation and weight remains arcane. After all, nobody sees God's face and lives.[4] The chosen prophet might be able to see His back, but the face is too luminous for mortals to fathom and survive. In due time, though; in due time.[5]

---

[4] Augustine becomes impatient and wonders when will be hear God's words again: the light of the divine face and the Word will illuminate us in due time: "Wilt Thou always remain silent? Even now, Thou deliverest from this deep abyss the Soul which seeks Thee, which thirsts after Thy delights, one whose 'heart says unto Thee: I have sought Thy face; Thy face, Lord, will I still seek'; for the soul is far from Thy face when it is in the dark realm of passion" (*Confessions* I.18.29).

[5] The challenge of seeing God's face and the meaning of the name on the forehead finds in Exodus 34 an extraordinary precursor. After having tempered God's wrath during the episode of the golden calf, Moses is invited to a moment of intimacy with God atop Mount Sinai. As the Lord dictates the text of the Tables to the prophet, something happens to Moses face: "he was there with the Lord forty days and forty nights; he neither ate bread nor drank water. And he wrote upon the tables the words of the covenant, the ten commandments. When Moses came down from Mount Sinai, with the two tables of the testimony in his hand as he came down from the mountain, Moses did not know that the skin of his face shone because he had been

When the Lamb offered Himself in redeeming holocaust for the forgiveness of sins, He rendered His law imitable. The Tablets of Stone were given a heart of flesh, according to the proverb; then, the heart of the law became living Word. The mirror, a symbol of an indirect and imperfect vision of God's face in the Pauline Epistles was destined to become a fundamental motif and literary genre in the medieval didactic tradition. In fact, most medieval books of Christian imitation are constructed in the form of specula. Saint Augustine was not only a pioneer in the fields of first-person and life-writing; his *Rule* is the first monastic rule in the West, but also a forerunner that contains its own, explicit methodology of specular exegesis: "These precepts should be read to you once a week, so that you will see yourselves in this little book as in a mirror and not neglect anything through forgetfulness. When you find yourselves doing what has been written here, thank the Lord, the giver of all good gifts" (*Praeceptum* VIII.2). Life is written on God's incarnated skin for us to be imitated. Given everyone's humble beginnings in matters of virtue, directly imitating God seemed like an unfeasible endeavor. Imitating God's human person in Christ, on the contrary, is a more approachable endeavor. However, He was one and perfect. We are many and imperfect.

The first imitators of Christ, the brothers and sisters partaking in the koinon of Jerusalem, had their imitation inscribed for our guidance in the Acts of the Apostles. In turn, Augustine writes a mirror of a mirror for us to be able to see God, no matter how far He may seem. God, the Father, may seem too great for us. God, the Son, at least resembles our skin and parameters to the point of making the rule not just obeyable, but also imitable. Christ is God's

---

talking with God. And when Aaron and all the people of Israel saw Moses, behold, the skin of his face shone, and they were afraid to come near him. But Moses called to them; and Aaron and all the leaders of the congregation returned to him, and Moses talked with them. And afterward all the people of Israel came near, and he gave them in commandment all that the Lord had spoken with him in Mount Sinai. And when Moses had finished speaking with them, he put a veil on his face; but whenever Moses went in before the Lord to speak with him, he took the veil off, until he came out; and when he came out, and told the people of Israel what he was commanded, the people of Israel saw the face of Moses, that the skin of Moses' face shone; and Moses would put the veil upon his face again, until he went in to speak with him" (Exodus 34:28–35).

Law morphed into an imitable model of individual life. Finally, the honest imitation of Christ's first followers embodies the first imitable model of communal life. Augustine's monastic wager is clear: the safest path to properly imitating Christ individually is the foundation of a house, maybe even a city, that supports our human finitude in the otherwise too colossal task of imitating God alone. Like Wittgenstein's ladder, however, the *Rule*'s mirror is one that wants—demands—to be discarded once it has fulfilled its purpose, which is the humble imitation of Christ's life in the original form adopted by His most direct followers at the Jerusalem koinon. Together, the first level of imitation will result in a sufficiently potent command of self, so that it allows us to venture into the final stage in direct vis-à-vis with God. Once ready to face Him, the mirror will be rendered superfluous and our foreheads will themselves become the mirrors on which God's Name will be reflected.

As beautiful as it is, the content of the *Rule* does not matter very much. What really matters is the why and how of the *Rule*. A rule is a mirror. Augustine himself would recognize that *all* he did was to draw the map to a treasure we knew and loved. The message inside the *Rule* is no different than Christ's superseding synthesis of the law as shared with the world on the Sermon of the Mount. Augustine said so himself when he composed a beautiful *Commentary on the Lord's Sermon on the Mount*: "If anyone piously and earnestly ponders the discourse which Our Lord Jesus Christ delivered on the Mount—as we read in the Gospel according to Matthew—I believe that he will find therein, with regards to good morals, the perfect standard of the Christian life" (*Commentary on the Lord's Sermon on the Mount* I.1). If we have been given a perfect script of life, why would a Christian rule of existence want to embrace any other set of principles? While the Tablets of Stone had been entrusted to Moses atop Mount Sinai, the tablets that found the New Covenant are not delivered in stone but spoken straight to the heart following the tradition of the book of Proverbs that is renewed on the Mount of Beatitudes:

Think not that I have come to abolish the law and the prophets; I have come not to abolish them but to fulfil them. For truly, I say to you, till heaven and earth pass away, not an iota, not a dot, will pass from the law until all is accomplished. Whoever then relaxes one of the least of these commandments and teaches men so, shall be called least in the kingdom of heaven; but he who does them and teaches them shall be called great in the kingdom of heaven. For I tell you, unless your righteousness exceeds that of the scribes and Pharisees, you will never enter the kingdom of heaven. (Matthew 5:17–20)

Augustine's rule of life does not add anything to Christ's sermon. Saint Augustine does not want to or need to alter the fundamental truth of the Scripture. The value of the *Rule* is the power of this little text to adapt the universal commandments into a simple table of house rules. Christ makes the law imitable; Augustine renders it an accessible and consuetudinary adaptation of the teaching of the Sermon on the Mount. The genius of the saint is the fact that he is capable of formulating a constitution that addresses brothers and sisters, which regulates their lives in a very detailed manner while preserving the simplicity of Christ's sermon. Christ had removed the casuistic of the law to prove its universality; then, Saint Augustine removes the casuistic normally involved in legal and philosophical texts regulating communities, societies, and laws. How is he able to do it? Because the *Rule*, which is truthfully not a very detailed document, contains both the fundamental commandments of Christian life and, as an original contribution, an exegetical clause that instructs us on how to read and adapt the rule to the infinite number of yet unforeseeable situations that without a doubt will emerge as a part of daily, human coexistence in the monastery: "The chief motivation for your sharing life together is to live harmoniously in the house and to have one heart and one soul seeking God" (*Praeceptum* I.1–2) and "The Lord grant you the grace to observe these precepts with love" (*Praeceptum* VIII.1–2). Every single article of the *Rule* is an application of this combination. On their own, the articles are just a convivial reformulation of the Sermon of the Mount and the communal life characterized in Acts of the Apostles 4:32–5. However, when read in combination with the first and last articles, they prepare the community for an endless number of situations. And they do so without diluting the message in casuistic legalese.

A simple example shall suffice. Immediately after the opening principle, Augustine explains his theory of apostolic property. He follows the steps of the Jerusalem koinon when he tells us: "Do not call anything your own; Possess everything in common [. . .] But on the other hand, those who enjoyed some measure of worldly success ought not to belittle their brothers who come to this holy society from a condition of poverty. They should endeavor to boast about the fellowship of poor brothers, rather that the social standing of rich relations" (*Praeceptum* I.7).[6] Acts, Sermon, and Rule are all imitable, followable, and obeyable. The difference is subtle but important: Christ is the rule, Acts is the imitation of the rule, and the monastic rule constitutes its transitive property of the fundamental Christian principle: "'You shall love the Lord your God with all your heart, and with all your soul, and with all your mind, and with all your strength.' The second is this, 'You shall love your neighbor as yourself.' There is no other commandment greater than these" (Mark 12:30–1). The generality of all three levels allows Augustine to write a rule not just intended for a North African house of coenobitism. On the contrary, he proves that it is worth imitating the apostles and Christ Himself. The *Rule* proves that the life resulting from that imitation is one worth pursuing. A life worth imitating.

* * *

Conclusion

Saint Augustine is the author of a timeless sermon. Entitled "Sermon 30 (80.) On the words of the Gospel, Matthew XVII. 'Why could not we cast him out, &c.' and on prayer," this little oration predictably exhorts the community to be good, but it does so in a most unpredictable manner:

And so, Brethren, we say, pray as much as ye are able. Evils abound, and God hath willed that evils should abound. Would that evil men did not abound, and then evils would not abound. Bad times! Troublesome times! This men are saying. Let our lives

---

[6]The volume that supplements this book is entirely focused on Augustine's theory of monastic property: "Et non dicatis aliquid proprium, sed sint uobis omnia communia [. . .] Sed rursus etiam illi qui aliquid esse uidebantur in saeculo non habeant fastidio fratres suos qui ad illam sanctam societatem ex paupertate uenerunt. Magis autem studeant, non de parentum diuitum dignitate, sed de pauperum fratrum societate, gloriari" (*Praeceptum* I.2–7).

be good; and the times are good. We make our times; such as we
are, such are the times. (236–44)[7]

We just love complaining about the times. This mortal chronology
of ours might seem irredeemably tainted, but Augustine helps us
realize that those maladies of the times are not something that
happens to us, but what happens with us instead. The *Rule* is a
manual that teaches how to make our times as good as they can be.
To do so, we must become so.

A rule is a mirror that looks beyond chronology to bring the
eternal into the temporal and the consuetudinary. It institutes an
imitation of God's absolute presence and makes everything wholly
present. Love remains, everything else flows away: "you will know
the extent of your progress as you enlarge your concern for the
common interest instead of your own private interest; enduring love
will govern all matters pertaining to the fleeting necessities of life"
(*Praeceptum* V.2). If our love is our weight, the more and higher we
love, the closer to eternity we will walk: the fleeting necessities of
life, this mortal chronology of ours, give way to a life of plenitude
in the presence of unconditional love.

Sub *specie aeternitatis*, the *Rule* is a narration of future acts that
God knew were bound to happen—prescience—but chose not to
determine to the letter—predestination. Midway, two of Augustine's
prime points of contention with the theological apparatus of
Western thought: grace—God's willingness to gratuitously save
humans even after the Fall—and Free Will—humanity's duty to
imitate Christ's love. From the human point of view, a rule entails
a call to action. A rulebook is not a book; it is a mirror where
the rules therein contained are not just instructions. Instruction
manuals tell us what to do. A monastic rule tells us why to do it.
The transformation provoked by God's Incarnation fulfills and
transcends the commandments of the law by transforming the

---

[7]While spurious quotations and translations abund, both the English translation
and Latin original are hard to track in contemporary publications. Luckily, Migne's
Patrologia Latina 38 includes a copy of the original "Sermo LXXX. *De verbis
Evangelii Matthei*, cap. XVII, 18–20, *Nos quare eum non potuimus ejicere? etc. Ubi
de oratione.*"

rules to be obeyed into rules to be imitated. Christ renders the law imitable.

Saint Augustine's *Rule* is not a book writing life, but a book proving that life is written. Written, yet free. The *Rule* is a manual on how to read the common textual fabric of human existence so that we as individuals can write a life of our own. In that vein, the pages in front of you compose a book writing about how life can be written and yet-to-be-written at once. Augustine's ultimate goal is the imitation of the original Jerusalem community portrayed in Acts of the Apostles 4:32–5. A koinonia of charity, selflessness, harmony, and unanimity. Of concord. The *Rule* begins with a call to action—love everyone—and ends with a quod erat demonstrandum clause: love begets love. If humans can recreate the heavenly city of New Jerusalem, we may be able to recreate the perfect life of the Imitable.

REFERENCES

Aaron, David H. (2006), *Etched in Stone: The Emergence of the Decalogue*, New York: T&T Clark.

Aristotle (1984), "*Metaphysics*," in Jonathan Barnes (ed.), *The Complete Works of Aristotle*, Princeton: Princeton University Press.

St. Augustine (1844), "Sermon 30 (80.) On the Words of the Gospel, Matthew XVII. 'Why Could Not We Cast Him Out, &C.' and On Prayer," in *Sermons on Selected Lessons of the New Testament*, 236–44, Oxford: John Henry Parker.

St. Augustine (1865), "Sermo LXXX. *De verbis Evangelii Matthei, cap. XVII, 18–20, Nos quare eum non potuimus ejicere? etc. Ubi de oratione*," in Jacques-Paul Migne (ed.), *Patrologia Latina 38, Sancti Aurelii Augustini, Opera Omnia*, 494–8, Paris: Garnier.

St. Augustine (1951), *Commentary on the Lord's Sermon on the Mount*, Washington: Catholic University of America Press.

St. Augustine (1959), *Sermons on the Liturgical Seasons*, Washington: Catholic University of America Press.

St. Augustine (1966), *Confessions*, Washington: Catholic University of America Press.

St. Augustine (1968a), *Retractations*, Washington: Catholic University of America Press.

St. Augustine (1968b), *The Teacher; the Free Choice of the Will; Grace and Free Will*, Washington: Catholic University of America Press.

St. Augustine (1986), *The Rule of Saint Augustine*, ed. Tarsicius J. Van Bavel, London: Image Books.

St. Augustine (1991), "*Praeceptum*," in George Lawless (ed.), *Augustine of Hippo and his Monastic Rule*, Oxford: Oxford University Press.

St. Augustine (1993), *Tractates on the Gospel of John 28–54*, Washington: Catholic University of America Press.

St. Augustine (2002), *Eighty-three Different Questions*, Washington: Catholic University of America Press.

St. Augustine (2008), *The City of God*, Washington: Catholic University of America Press.

St. Augustine (2010), "*On Christian Teaching*," in William Harmless (ed.), *Augustine in His Own Words*, Washington: Catholic University of America Press.

St. Basil of Caesarea (2004), "The Long Rules," in McMillan, Douglas J. and Daniel Marcel La Corte (eds), *Regular Life: Monastic, Canonical, and Mendicant Rules*, 35–42, Kalamazoo: Medieval Institute.

Van Bavel, Tarsicius J., ed. (1986), *The Rule of Saint Augustine [RA]*, London: Image Books.

Benjamin, Walter (1968), "Theses on the Philosophy of History," in Hannah Arendt and Harry Zohn (eds), *Illuminations*, New York: Schocken Books.

Berlin, Isaiah (1969), *Two Concepts of Liberty*, Oxford: Oxford University Press.

Butler, Alban (1990), *Lives of the Saints I*, Westminster: Christian Classics.

Descartes, René (1894), *Discours de la méthode*, Paris: Bibliotheque Nationale.

Enuma Elis (2013), in Wilfred G. Lambert (ed.), *Babylonian Creation Myths*, Winona Lake: Eisenbrauns.

Fuss, Peter (1986), "Rousseau's Engagement with Amour-Propre," *Journal of Political and Social* X (3): 101–13.

Hammurabi (2005), "*Hammurabi's Laws*," in M. E. J. Richardson (ed.), *Hammurabi's Laws: Text, Translation and Glossary*, 28–135, London: Bloomsbury.

Hesiod (1988), *Theogony. Works and Days*, Oxford: Oxford University Press.

Hollingworth, Miles (2013), *Saint Augustine of Hippo. An Intellectual Biography*, Oxford: Oxford University Press.

Hollingworth, Miles (2018), *Ludwig Wittgenstein*, Oxford: Oxford University Press.

The Holy Bible (1966), *Revised Standard Version Catholic Edition*, San Francisco: Ignatius Press.

Josephus, Flavius (1737), *The Works of Flavius Josephus*, London: Fielding and Walker.

Kaufmann, Yehezkel (1961), *The Religion of Israel, from Its Beginnings to the Babylonian Exile*, London: George Allen & Unwin.

Lambert, Wilfred G. (2013), *Babylonian Creation Myths*, Winona Lake: Eisenbrauns.

Lawless, George (1991), *Augustine of Hippo and his Monastic Rule*, Oxford: Oxford University Press.

Lejeune, Philippe (1975), *Le pacte autobiographique*, Paris: Seuil.

McMillan, Douglas J. and Daniel Marcel La Corte, eds (2004), *Regular Life: Monastic, Canonical, and Mendicant. Rules*, Kalamazoo: Medieval Institute.

Migne, Jacques-Paul (1865), *Patrologia Latina 38, Sancti Aurelii Augustini, Opera Omnia*, Paris: Garnier.

Pârvan, Alexandra (2017), "Revelation 20:12-15: Augustine on the 'book of life,' and the conflicting picture of predestination in *De civitate dei* 20,14–15," *Zeitschrift für Antikes Christentum / Journal of Ancient Christianity* 21 (3): 472–95.

Philo of Alexandria (1997), *The Works of Philo*, Peabody: Hendrickson.

Plato (1980), *The Collected Dialogues of Plato*, Princeton: Princeton University Press.

Plutarch (1914), *Plutarch's Lives* London: MacMillian.

Putnam, Hilary (1999), *Reason, Truth, and History*, Cambridge: Cambridge University Press.

The Qur'an: A New Translation by M.A.S Abdel Haleem, (2005) Oxford: Oxford University Press.

Ratzinger, Joseph (1957), "Originalität und Überlieferung in Augustins Begriff der *confessio*," *Revue d'Études Augustiniennes et Patristiques* 3 (4): 375–92.

Rousseau, Jean-Jacques (1782), *Les Confessions*, London: Neuchâtel.

Rousseau, Jean-Jacques (2002), "Discourse on the Origin and Foundations of Inequality Among Mankind," in *The Social Contract and The First and Second Discourses*, New Haven: Yale University Press.

Spinoza (2007), *Ethica*, Madrid: Alianza.

Strong, James (1890), *The Exhaustive Concordance of the Bible*, New York: Eaton & Mains.

Trinkaus Zagzebski, Linda (1991), *The Dilemma of Freedom and Foreknowledge*, New York: Oxford University Press.

Verheijen, Luc (1967), *La règle de Saint Augustin*, Paris: Études Augustiniennes.

Verheijen, Luc (1979), *Saint Augustine's Monasticism in the Light of Acts 4.32-35*, Wetteren: Cultura Press-Villanova University Press.

Verheijen, Luc (1980), *Nouvelle approche de la règle de Saint Augustin*, Bégrolles en Mauges: Abbaye de Bellefontaine.

Wittgenstein, Ludwig (1961), *Tractatus Logico-Philosophicus*, London: Routledge.

Wittgenstein, Ludwig (1986), *Philosophical Investigations*, Oxford: Blackwell.

Zumkeller, Adolar, and Andreas E. J. Grote (2018), *Das Mönchtum des Heiligen Augustinus*, Würzburg: Cassiciacum-Augustinus bei Echter.

INDEX